Religion in focus

Judaism

in today's world

Vivienne Cato

Claire Clinton

Sally Lynch

Janet Orchard

Deborah Weston

Angela Wright

John Murray

Other titles in this series:
Christianity in today's world ISBN 0 7195 7193 6
Islam in today's world ISBN 0 7195 7194 4

Biblical quotations

Bible excerpts have been taken from THE TANAKH – the holy
scriptures. The new JPS translation according to the traditional
Hebrew text, Copyright 1985 by the Jewish Publication Society.
Used by permission.

Other sources

In this book you will also find many contemporary statements
about Jewish beliefs. These are the views of ordinary Jews. They
would not necessarily be seen as authoritative by all Jews.

Note: Words printed in SMALL CAPITALS (first mention only) are
defined in the Glossary on pages 120–21.

Many of the words used by Jews are Hebrew words. Hebrew
uses a different alphabet, so you may find that these words are
written in English in different ways. In addition, Hebrew has a
throaty sound like that found in the Scottish word 'lo*ch*', or the
name of the composer, 'Ba*ch*'.

With thanks to

Many members of the Jewish faith community in Britain and
representatives of many different Jewish organisations have been
consulted in the preparation of this book. However, the authors
take full responsibility for the views expressed herein. The
authors would particularly like to acknowledge the helpful advice
of the following:

Ronnie Cohen; Steve Derby, Education Officer for Tzedek;
Reverend Jonathan Gorsky, Education Advisor for the Council of
Christians and Jews; Clive Lawton, Trustee of Tzedek; Lynndy
Levine; Roger Owen, former Chief Examiner at GCSE; Rabbi
Sybil Sheridan, Rabbi of the Thames Valley Progressive
Community, Reading and lecturer at the Leo Baeck College,
London; Dr Alan Unterman, Minister of the Yeshurun Synagogue,
Manchester and Lecturer in Comparative Religions at the
University of Manchester and Rabbi Jonathan Wittenberg of the
New North London Synagogue.

© Vivienne Cato, Claire Clinton, Sally Lynch, Janet Orchard, Deborah Weston, Angela Wright 2001

First published 2001
by Hodder Murray
50 Albemarle Street
London W1S 4BD

Reprinted 2002, 2005

Artwork by Oxford Illustrators Ltd, Edward Ripley
Layouts by Fiona Webb
Colour separations by Colourscript, Mildenhall, Suffolk
Typeset in Rockwell Light by Wearset, Boldon, Tyne and Wear
Printed and bound in Spain by Bookprint S.L., Barcelona

A CIP catalogue record for this book is available from the British Library.

ISBN 0 7195 7197 9
Teacher's Book ISBN 0 7195 7433 1

Contents

A
Introduction

B
Thinking
about morality

C
Thinking
about God

Acknowledgements

The authors and publishers are grateful to the following for permission to include material in the text:

Bible excerpts throughout are from *THE TANAKH: The New JPS Translation According to the Traditional Hebrew Text*. Copyright 1985 by the Jewish Publication Society. Used by permission; **p.24** *tr* from *To be a Jewish woman* © Dr Lisa Aiken 1995, published by J Aronson 1995; *br* Rabbi Dr Jonathan Sacks, Chief Rabbi; **p.25** Professor Robert Winston; **p.28** *tl* from *To be a Jewish woman* © Dr Lisa Aiken 1995, published by J Aronson 1995; *bl* from *Faith and Practice: a guide to Reform Judaism* by Rabbi Dr Jonathan Romain, published by The Reform Synagogues of Great Britain; **p.37** letters by Samuel Hugo Bergmann and others, from *The Seventh Million: the Israelis and the Holocaust* © Tom Segev, translation © Haim Watzman, published by Hill & Wang; **pp.46–7, 48** from *Kosher sex* © Shmuley Boteach 1998, published by Gerald Duckworth & Co. Ltd.; **p.49** by Rabbi Dr Jonathan Sacks, from guidelines issued by the Marriage Authorisation Office of the Chief Rabbi; **p.51** Rabbi Nina Beth Cardin; **p.53** from the *Jewish Chronicle* 18/3/94; **p.58** from *The Big Book of Jewish Humor* © William Novak 1981, published by HarperCollins in the US; **p.61** from *The Big Book of Jewish Humor* © William Novak 1981, published by HarperCollins in the US; **p.63** Alan N. Canton; Vice President; Adams-Blake Publishing; www.adams-blake.com; **p.71** from *The Big Book of Jewish Humor* © William Novak 1981, published by HarperCollins in the US; **p.90** from *Yitzhak Rabin, Soldier of Peace*, first published by Peter Halban Publishers 1996, copyright © 1996 by the Jerusalem Report; **p.91** Neve Shalom School for Peace; **p.101** Dr C. Benton, Texas, USA from his website; **p.106** Interview extracts from *A life apart: Hasidism in America*; **p.107** from *This is for everyone* © Rabbi Douglas Goldhamer and Melissa Stengel 1999, published by Larson Publications; **p.108** Interview with Felicity Kendall by Danny Danziger, from the *Mail on Sunday*; **p.110–11** based on *Leon Greenman, Auschwitz Survivor 98288 – A Resource for Holocaust Education* published by The Jewish Museum to accompany their permanent exhibition about Leon Greenman. See Teacher's Resource Book for more information; **p.112** *tl* from *After Auschwitz: history, theology and contemporary Judaism* © Richard L. Rubenstein updated 1992, published by The Johns Hopkins University Press; *tr* from *With God in Hell: Judaism in the ghettos and death camps*, by Eliezer Berkovits, Sanhedrin Press, New York, 1979; *bl* by Emil Fackenheim: source unknown; *br* from *Night* © Elie Wiesel, translated from the French by Stella Rodway; **p.116** 'A Vision of the Future' by Judy Chicago Merger © Aleph, P'nai Or Religious Fellowship, Philadelphia, USA.

Illustration acknowledgements

Cover: Yael Braun/Camera Press; **p.1** *tl* Sally Lynch, *tr* Calligraphy by Vetta Alexis, *br* Ted Spiegel/Topham Picturepoint; **p.2** *t* Lynndy Levin, *bl* Anne Krisman, *bc* Avigail Cohen, *br* Dan Reinhold; **p.3** *t* Reverend Jonathan Gorsky, *bl* Nikki and Rabbi Paul Glantz, *bc* Ronnie Cohen, *br* Talya Baker; **p.4** *tl* Lynndy Levin, *c* John Townson/Creation; **p.4-5** Nils Jorgensen/Rex Features; **p.5** *t* & *br* John Townson/Creation; **p.14** Daniel Rose; **p.15** Maggie Murray/Format; **p.18** page from Tractate Megillah, Talmud Bavli, Schottenstein Edition, The Artscroll Series, © Mesorah Publications 1991; **p.25** Caroline Mardon/Rex Features; **p.26** *t* & *b* photos by David Silverman © 2000/Sonia Halliday Photographs; **p.27** *tl* & *b* photos by David Silverman © 2000/Sonia Halliday Photographs, *tr* Ronnie Cohen; **p.32** The North London Hospice; **p.34** *t* Popperfoto, *b* © Bettmann/Corbis; **p.38** *tl* Petit Format/Nestlé/Science Photo Library, *tr* Topham Picturepoint, *b* Rex Features; **p.39** Calligraphy by Vetta Alexis; **p.40** *tl* © David H. Wells/Corbis, *bl* © Ted Spiegel/Corbis, *r* photo by David Silverman © 2000/Sonia Halliday Photographs; **p.41** *l* photo by Elana Ripps for AVODAH, *r* photo by David Silverman © 2000/Sonia Halliday Photographs; **p.43** Rabbi Dr Jonathan Romain; **p.44** *t, bl* & *br* © Ted Spiegel/Corbis; **p.45** *tl* © Richard T. Nowitz/Corbis, *tr* © Annie Griffiths Belt/Corbis, *b* Vetta Alexis; **p.46** William Conran/Camera Press; **p.47** 'Amour' by Andre Rouillard, Superstock; **p.49** PA News Photo Library; **p.51** Topham Picturepoint; **p.53** Topham Picturepoint; **p.54** photo by David Silverman © 2000/Sonia Halliday Photographs; **p.55** © Ted Spiegel/Corbis; **p.59** *l* AKG London, *r* David Hoffman/Rex Features; **p.61** reproduced courtesy of the Community Security Trust; **p.63** Rich Pedroncelli/Associated Press; **p.65** *tl* photo by Leah Volynsky for AVODAH, *tr* AVODAH, *bl* photo by David Rosenn for AVODAH, *br* photo by Amy Reich for AVODAH; **p.66** *t* © Annie Griffiths Belt/Corbis, *b* PA News Photo Library; **p.67** Peter Till; **p.68** Reproduced courtesy of JNF (photo: John Townson/Creation); **p.71** © John Caldwell; **p.72** *t* World Jewish Relief, *b* Sipa Press/Rex Features; **p.73** World Jewish Relief; **p.74** *t* & *b* Tzedek; **p.75** Tzedeck; **p.76** photo by David Silvermann © 2000/ Sonia Halliday Photographs; **p.78** reproduced with permission of Punch Ltd; **p.80** Vivienne Cato; **p.81** *t* The Noah Project, *b* Vivienne Cato; **p.83** © Philip Gould/Corbis; **p.85** a prize-winning entry in Bible 2000; **p.88** 'They shall beat their swords into ploughshares' from *The Times* 27 September 1996 © Peter Brookes/ Times Newspapers Limited, 1996; **p.89** Popperfoto; **p.90** *t* Levine/Sipa Press/Rex Features, *b* photo by David Silverman © 2000/Sonia Halliday; **p.92** *t* Sally Lynch, *c* Gilles Corniere/Still Pictures, *b* Sally Lynch; **p.95** *t* photo by David Silverman © 2000/Sonia Halliday Photographs, *b* © Ted Spiegel/Corbis; **p.96** *tl* AKG London, *bl* Private Collection/Bridgeman Art Library, London, *r* British Library, London/Bridgeman Art Library, London; **p.97** *l* AKG London © ADAGP, Paris & DACS, London 2000, *r* Private Collection/Bridgeman Art Library, London; **p.101** © Harold Taylor ABIPP/Oxford Scientific Films; **p.102** *background* John Townson/Creation, *inset* © Roger Ressmeyer/Corbis; **p.104** © Ted Spiegel/Corbis; **p.105** *tl* © Ted Spiegel/Corbis, *tr* Simon O'Connor, *b* Marc Michaels; **p.106** © David H. Wells/Corbis; **p.107** John Townson/Creation; **p.108** © Hugh Thompson/Capital Pictures; **p.109** Daniel Fitzpatrick in the St. Louis Post-Dispatch; **p.110** *t* The Jewish Museum, London, *b* AKG London; **p.111** *l* AKG London, *r* The Jewish Museum, London; **p.117** *t* AKG London, *b* Sally Lynch.

t = top, *l* = left, *r* = right, *b* = bottom, *c* = centre

While every effort has been made to contact copyright holders, the publishers apologise for any omissions, which they will be pleased to rectify at the earliest opportunity.

UNIT 1

A Jewish world view

שמע ישראל יהוה אלהינו יהוה אחד:

Hear, O Israel: the Lord our God, the Lord is One.

The opening of the SHEMA (Deuteronomy 6.4)

The Shema is said twice every day by Orthodox Jews. A copy of the Shema written on parchment is placed inside a decorated case and attached to the doorposts of a Jewish home. This is called a MEZUZAH (see photo above). The Shema is also put into small leather boxes that men strap to their forehead and arms for weekday morning prayers. These are called TEPHILIN (right).

The words of the Shema are probably 3000 years old. But for Jews today they are relevant and living. The Shema expresses some of Jews' most important ideas about God and each person's relationship with God. You can read more of it on page 2.

Through the rest of this book you are going to find out more about what Jews believe about God and how they attempt to put the Shema into practice in daily life.

1.1 What does the Shema mean to Jews?

There are 300,000 Jews in Britain today, mostly living in the major cities. Some you could spot by the way they dress, but you would only know others were Jewish if they chose to tell you. We asked some what the Shema means to them.

> When I say the first sentence of the Shema, I cover my eyes with my right hand. I think deeply into the words and I sense a tremendous unity, God's oneness in the world. I feel whole and I feel humble.

> The Shema is a powerful and clear prayer . . . I always feel a link with the whole Jewish community when I hear it . . . it is a bonding prayer, showing there is a core of belief which all Jewish people share.

A

Hear, O Israel! The Lord our God, the Lord is One. You shall love the Lord your God with all your heart and with all your soul and with all your might. Take to heart these instructions with which I charge you this day. Impress them upon your children. Recite them when you stay at home and when you are away, when you lie down and when you get up. Bind them as a sign on your hand and let them serve as a symbol on your forehead; inscribe them on the doorposts of your house and on your gates.

The complete first paragraph of the Shema (Deuteronomy 6.4–9)

Lynndy Levin (see page 4) is an ORTHODOX Jew living in north-west London. Orthodox means keeping to Jewish traditions. Her husband is a RABBI, and she plays an active role in their synagogue.

Anne Krisman is a REFORM Jew living in East London. Reform means adapting Jewish traditions for the modern world. She is a teacher and is very involved with local inter-faith groups.

> The Shema defines the uniqueness of the Jewish people: only we are commanded to worship God in that way. It also defines our responsibilities towards God and the rest of mankind. Saying the Shema gives me the feeling that there's always someone watching over me and I'm constantly being protected. This is why I recite it twice daily.

> At the heart of every belief or religion is a prayer or mantra. For me, this is the Shema. The few moments it takes to recite it are the best opportunities I have in a busy day to take time to reflect on my Jewishness and express my beliefs in my own personal way.

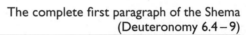

Avigail Cohen is an ultra-Orthodox Jew living in north-west London. After school she spent a year studying Jewish texts and issues in Israel. She is now at university in London, studying to become an occupational therapist.

Dan Reinhold lives in north London and works in marketing. He is a member of an Orthodox synagogue.

ACTIVITY

Copy and complete this chart to analyse what these people are saying about the Shema. You won't be able to complete all the columns for every speaker.

Name	How they use it	Ideas or beliefs it conveys to them	Feelings

DISCUSS

1 The Shema instructs Jews to love God with all their heart, soul and might. What do you think this means?
2 Give examples of how someone could do this in practice. (You can get some ideas from these two pages.)
3 Do you think it is harder or easier for Jews to love God today than it was thousands of years ago when the Shema was first written? Give reasons.

When I say the Shema I become aware of God who is One, beyond any form of physical being or human comprehension and is the Creator of all things. As we contemplate the Divine we are to develop a sense of love which will be given with heart and soul and asks of us all that we possess. This is the well-spring of our religious life.

Jonathan Gorsky is Education Advisor for the Council of Christians and Jews. He is an Orthodox Jew.

The words of the Shema are a meditation. I find endless meaning in the words 'love your God with all your heart and all your soul and all your might.' They say to me that to love God is to engage in the world, by carrying out all our actions and relationships with our whole being, which includes our thinking, feeling and willing.

To me, the Shema is both a statement about the nature of God and also a daily reminder to try and live my life by the ethical and moral values embodied within Judaism, and to encourage my children to do the same.

I'm not Orthodox, and I don't recite the Shema every day. But I have a mezuzah on my doorposts and will teach the Shema to my children. It's a powerful prayer because it begins with some quite abstract ideas about God's relationship to the Jewish people, but then links them strongly to small events in everyone's daily life.

Nikki Glantz is a social worker in Hertfordshire. She recently married Paul (see page 104). At the wedding she circled him seven times under the wedding canopy, a traditional Jewish ritual symbolising that they are tying their lives together.

Ronnie Cohen is a MASORTI Jew (see page 12). He studies Jewish texts regularly and is an active participant at his synagogue, where he leads many services. He is Talya Baker's father.

Talya Baker is a Masorti Jew living in St Albans. She attends synagogue most weeks and for festivals. She worked as an editor on this book.

1.2 What does Shabbat mean to Jews?

You will quickly see that tradition – doing things the way they have always been done – is very important in Judaism. One of the central, unifying traditions is SHABBAT: the Jewish Sabbath. This comes every week as a reminder of God's Creation, and a time for Jews to concentrate on the spiritual aspects of life.

Shabbat begins on Friday night, an important time for Jews everywhere. It is a time for family and friends to eat together and be together. They light candles, bless bread and wine, say Shabbat prayers and sing songs to separate this day from the rest of the week.

An Orthodox Friday night

Lynndy Levin is a consultant in Jewish education. Her husband is the rabbi of a synagogue in north-west London. She is the rebbetzin – this simply means 'rabbi's wife', but, especially in traditional communities, it is often a demanding community role. Lynndy is Orthodox. Here she describes a traditional Friday night in her home and how she prepares for it.

A Reform Friday night could be different, as you can see from the notes around the edge.

A Reform Friday night

> In my family we all work. We aren't Orthodox, so we don't stop work early on a Friday. We usually begin our Shabbat at about 8p.m., whatever time the sun sets.

> We sometimes walk to synagogue, as it helps to get us 'in the Shabbat mood', but depending on the weather, and how much time we've got, we drive sometimes or don't go at all.

> We believe it is OK to cook as necessary on Shabbat, so we don't leave the oven on.

Friday daytime is called 'EREV Shabbat', the day which heralds the approaching Shabbat. In the Creation story each day begins in the evening, so Shabbat 'comes in' about half an hour before sunset on Friday evening. By then, all preparations must be complete, and that's why the day leading up to the Shabbat or festival becomes almost part of it in focus and atmosphere.

Each Friday morning I try to bake my own CHALLOT (sweet braided loaves). If I can't, it's easy to buy tasty ones at one of the several Jewish bakeries around. Somehow though, homebaked CHALLAH is best and the smell as it bakes is both a tantalizing and absolutely Shabbat-like fragrance! One portion must be ritually separated from the dough before it is braided and baked. As the piece of dough is separated we say a special blessing which acknowledges G-d (see Checkpoint on page 94) as the source of all blessing. It shows

our awareness that by performing His commandments (in this case by separating the dough), we enhance our spiritual connection.

Soon the house is filled with the wonderful aroma of many other traditional Shabbat foods, including for lunch next day, a dish called 'cholent', which is like a casserole of meat, beans and potatoes. This will be left to keep warm on the stove, the low flame of which will be covered with a sheet of metal called a 'blech' (Yiddish word) which covers both the flame and the controls of the stove, as no cooking is allowed over the entire Shabbat.

The children come home from school and my husband from work. Everyone feels the unmistakable excitement and atmosphere of Erev Shabbat which is so special.

The house is sparkling. The table is set and in its centre are the shining Shabbat candlesticks with white candles in them ready for lighting at sundown.

Everyone is dressed in their Shabbat best. Mums and daughters gather round the candles, dads and sons go off to the synagogue. Of course, women and girls can go to synagogue too if they want to, after they have lit the candles. No driving on Shabbat though.

Lighting the candles on Shabbat is an incredibly spiritual time. Outside the daylight is waning, it's a quiet and reflective time of day. Just before candle-lighting there is a custom to give a coin to charity.

At a time when we are so full of joy we want to remember those who are less fortunate. Then the match is struck, the candles lit and before the blessing is said three circular movements are made over the candles as if to draw the Shabbat in. With our hands covering our eyes we say the blessing and then think deeply into ourselves and whisper our own private prayer. This is such a lovely sharing time which brings mums, daughters, grans, friends and guests close in the warmth and beauty of the moment. In fact, I often think as I light the candles that Jewish women all over the globe do the same thing, and that gives a wonderful feeling of unity.

On returning from the synagogue warm greetings of SHABBAT SHALOM (peace be to you on the Sabbath) are exchanged. Often there are guests – some expected and some unexpected. Hospitality is a great feature of the Jewish home. Songs are sung to the angels who are said to accompany us home from the synagogue, to the woman of the house and metaphorically to the land of Israel and to the TORAH.

Then the man of the house makes KIDDUSH (sanctification) over a goblet of red wine of which everyone at the table has a sip. The words of Kiddush are from Genesis 1.31 and 2.3 and celebrate the completion of the six days of the Creation and the resting from creating.

Following the Kiddush everyone washes their hands in a ritual way using a large two-handled cup. A blessing is made over the hands and then they are carefully dried. There is no more speaking until the blessing has been made over the challah and we have taken our first mouthful of the challah. The silence between the washing and the eating is to connect the two as sanctified or spiritual actions which remind us that G-d is the Creator of the universe and brings forth bread from the ground. Our eating is not just to fill our hungry stomachs, it is also a spiritual eating done with awareness, sensitivity and dignity.

Then the meal is served. It is joyous and full of chat. Shabbat songs are sung, words of Torah are shared and children are encouraged to show what they know. Sometimes there are deep and interesting discussions lasting long into the night. It is quality time, a time of connection, communication and inclusion.

After the meal is over, the grace after meals is sung by everyone together to thank G-d for His bounty, protection and nurture, and to ensure that we take nothing for granted.

> It's not always a man who makes Kiddush at our Friday night.

1. Choose three elements of Lynndy's Friday night that most appeal to you and three that least appeal. Explain your choices.
2. Some Jews believe it is important to continue observing these Shabbat traditions in exactly the same way. Others adapt traditions to the family's situation. Why do you think there are these different approaches?
3. What are the advantages of each approach?

SAVE AS...

Do you expect your study of Judaism to be helpful or relevant for your own life?

Write a paragraph recording your ideas about the relevance of Judaism to your life. Later, when you have explored how Jews apply their beliefs to some issues facing them in the modern world, you will see if your views have changed at all.

> We talk over the meal, but sometimes watch television later on.

> We don't usually do grace after meals.

1.3 A cartoon history of Judaism

History is very important to understanding Judaism because the shared history of the Jewish people is what unites them. In this course you will see that beliefs about God and about moral issues can differ dramatically from Jew to Jew, but all Jews share a common past and seek guidance and inspiration from the same texts.

So, here is a short history of Judaism. As you read through this you will find some ideas highlighted like this. You can find out more about these on page 10.

ACTIVITY

Frames 6, 10, and 16 each have an empty bubble. On a separate sheet of paper, write what that person might be thinking or saying.

PHASE 1: The foundations – 2000BCE to 900BCE

Approx. 2000BCE (BCE means Before Christian Era. The dates are the same as BC.)
1.   God made a covenant with Abraham. God would bless Abraham. Abraham would worship only the one God.

Go forth from your native land and from your father's house to the land that I will show you. I will make of you a great nation, and I will bless you. I will make your name great, and you shall be a blessing . . . [for] all the families of the earth.

CANAAN

EGYPT

2.   Abraham moved his family to Canaan. Just as God had promised, his descendants did well. Things were looking good. But then disaster struck. There was a terrible famine in Canaan. Abraham's grandson Jacob (also called Israel) moved the family to Egypt for refuge.

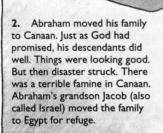

Approx. 1500BCE
3.   Abraham's descendants (there were now thousands of them, known as Israelites) were made slaves by Pharaoh.

Approx. 1300BCE
4.   God sent Moses to lead the Israelites out of Egypt. Moses tried persuasion first. Then God sent terrible plagues, including blood, frogs and boils.

Let my people go.

If you get rid of these frogs, I'll let your people go.

5.   After every plague, Pharaoh went back on his word. The tenth plague was the death of the first-born son of each Egyptian household. But the Israelites were spared. Pharaoh ordered the Israelites to leave.

I'll send my soldiers to catch them later.

6. With God's help, the Israelites escaped across the Red Sea into the desert. On Mount Sinai God gave Moses the Ten Commandments telling them how to live. They told them to worship only the One God.

7. When Moses died Joshua took over. He led the Israelites back into their 'promised land', Canaan, after forty years in the desert and by 1000BCE Israel had become a strong nation, with its own king, its own laws and a spectacular temple built by Solomon. This was the focal point of worship, where God was worshipped and sacrifices were performed. It was as if the promise to Abraham had been fulfilled. But would it last?

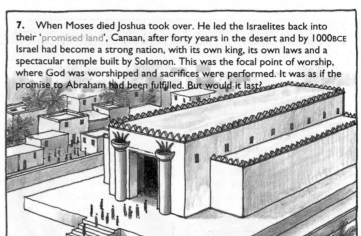

PHASE 2: Rebuilding Temple-based worship – 900BCE to 70CE

Approx. 900BCE

8. After King Solomon's death Israel split into two nations. There was idol-worship, rivalry and civil war. God's commandments were forgotten. Prophets warned of impending disaster.

Worship the One God or you'll be sorry.

586BCE

9. Foreign armies marched in. They destroyed the Temple and took the leaders of Israel away into exile.

Why has this happened?

Because you disobeyed God. But don't despair. Return to God and you will be blessed again.

God will send a Messiah – an anointed ruler – who will bring in a new age of peace and justice on Earth.

444BCE

10. Some Jews were allowed to return to Israel. They started to rebuild Jerusalem. The rebuilt Temple became the centre of Jewish life and people began teaching and interpreting the oral Torah. Very little of Judaism had yet been written down; the Law was still mainly oral.

Meanwhile in exile ...

Many Jews did not return to Israel from exile. In Babylon and in other countries they developed their own religious life away from the Temple.

7

PHASE 3: The Jews disperse – 70CE to the 18th century

11. In 70CE the Temple was destroyed again, this time by the armies of the Roman Empire. Judaism again lost its focal point. The oral teachings of Judaism were finally written down. From this time on, Judaism focused on Torah, synagogues and local communities, rather than the Temple in Jerusalem. Rabbis – or teachers (see page 106) – were especially important in the development of Jewish tradition from this time.

12. The Jews dispersed all over the world. This movement was called the diaspora. Wherever the Jews settled, they took their rituals and traditions with them. Some lived as religious communities separated from those around them. Many dreamed of one day returning to the land of Israel.

ROME

ISRAEL

NORTH AFRICA

EGYPT

ARABIAN DESERT

TO INDIA

13. In the countries where they settled, Jews often encountered prejudice, either because of religion or simply because they were different. In medieval Europe, from the eleventh century, some Christian leaders encouraged hatred by saying that the Jews were responsible for killing Jesus. All over western and central Europe envy, suspicion and hatred spilled into persecution and murder.

This is William of Newburgh reporting from York, England in March 1190. The mob trapped the Jews in York Castle. They gave the Jews a choice – to become Christians or be massacred. Some Jews killed themselves. The rest were burned or butchered by the mob.

PHASE 4: Diversity in Judaism – the 18th century to the present

14. From the eighteenth century, attitudes to Jews begin to change in some countries; for example, in France after the French Revolution Jews were allowed to vote. The barriers between Jew and Gentile (non-Jew) were gradually broken down and some Jews became influential members of society. In other countries, particularly in eastern Europe, Jews lived in poverty and faced constant persecution. When Jews were admitted to Gentile societies, they debated how to respond...

> The Jews need to keep **separate**. The modern Gentile world has nothing for us. It will destroy our faith and our traditions.

> I disagree. We can **share** in Gentile society, but we must keep the essential traditions of Judaism.

> The world is changing and many of our traditions are no longer relevant. Let's **reform** Judaism in the light of modern progress.

As a result, different Jewish communities developed in different directions. Judaism became a diverse religion with several different strands. You can find out more about this on page 12.

15. When Hitler became leader of Germany in 1933 he started the most horrific period of persecution the Jewish people had ever known. Hitler had a fanatical hatred of Jews. Jews in Germany were abused, attacked and finally, amid the horrors of World War Two, systematically worked to death or murdered throughout German-held territory. Six million European Jews were killed in the Holocaust or SHOAH.

16. Down the ages traditional Jews believed that at the end of time they would return to the land of Israel, which had been promised to Abraham by God. This hope remained central to Jewish prayer. A small community of Jews always lived in the land, and the suffering and poverty of nineteenth-century Jewry gave birth to the Zionist movement, which wanted to return to the land of Israel. The terrible destruction of the Holocaust brought them many supporters and in 1948 the State of Israel was created. Since then, Jews have moved there from all over Europe, Russia, the USA and north Africa.

Big ideas

In the cartoon history some of the big ideas are highlighted. On this page you can find out more about them.

One God

Judaism is a monotheistic religion. Jews believe there is one God, the creator of the universe, who is both beyond this world, and within it. In Unit 5 you will look at this in more detail.

Torah

This is the original sacred text of Judaism, on which all other Jewish texts are based. It is the highest source of authority for Jews. You will find out more about it on page 16, and about how Jews use it throughout this book.

Commandments

The MITZVOT, or commandments, were given to Moses. As well as the Ten Commandments there are another 603 that Jews have to follow. Jewish faith is a life of obedience to the law of the Lord. One purpose of the mitzvot is to keep society stable and to protect the individual from exploitation. But their main purpose is to encourage spiritual awareness. The commandments emphasise people's personal responsibilities before God. The term MITZVAH (plural, mitzvot) is also used to refer to any good deed, as a good deed is always the will of God.

The branches of Judaism differ in how literally they believe Jews today have to obey these commandments. More about this on page 19.

A covenant

Jews believe that this one God formed a special relationship with Abraham – called a covenant. Abraham's descendants are the heirs of that special relationship. A covenant has two sides. God's side of the covenant is to instruct and bless the Jews. The Jews' side of the covenant is to obey the one true God and God's commandments.

COVENANT

ONE GOD

RITUALS & TRADITIONS

TORAH

HOLOCAUST/ SHOAH

COMMANDMENTS

DIASPORA

PROMISED LAND/ ISRAEL

Promised land/Israel

Moses led the Jewish people out of Egypt towards the 'promised land' of Canaan. They lived there for centuries until wars spread them far and wide. In 1948 the modern State of Israel was created in the area that had been Canaan. Jews today are divided in their views on modern Israel. Some see the area as having religious significance – they see the modern State of Israel as the fulfilment of a 2000-year-old dream. Others value it simply as a place for Jews to live without persecution. Many Jews are concerned about the situation in Israel, where tension between Jews and Palestinians is an uncomfortable feature of everyday life.

Rituals and traditions

From its early roots Judaism has inherited many rituals: there are weekly rituals surrounding the Sabbath; there is an annual cycle of festivals through the year. For example, Pesach (the Passover) is observed each year by Jews all over the world. These festivals and the historical events that lie behind them are central parts of being Jewish. Many Jews who would not describe themselves as 'religious' celebrate some of these festivals, though the ways in which different Jews mark any event will differ greatly. You can see examples of this on pages 4, 76 and 102.

Holocaust/Shoah

The Holocaust (which Jews often call the 'Shoah') wiped out two-thirds of Jews in Europe. Today still, it affects the attitudes of Jews to many issues and it also affects the attitudes of non-Jews to Jews. In this book you will find that the Shoah appears at many points as a factor affecting Judaism, in particular in its impact on attitudes to racism (pages 56 and 61) and belief about God (page 112).

Diaspora

Most Jews live in the diaspora (outside Israel) – there are more Jews in the USA than in Israel! Jews everywhere have adapted to and influenced the societies around them and have become thoroughly integrated into many cultures.

ACTIVITY A

Draw up a table like this and use the explanations on page 10 to summarise in your own words each of the key ideas from the cartoon history.

Frame	Idea	Your summary
1/6	One God	
1	Covenant	
6	Commandments	
7/16	Promised land/Israel	
10	Torah	
12	Diaspora	
12	Rituals and traditions	
15	Holocaust/Shoah	

ACTIVITY B

1 a) Summarise each statement in Source A on a separate card.
  b) Sort the cards into categories:

  • beliefs you hold
  • beliefs you don't hold.

2 Now sort them into different categories:
  a) qualities of God
  b) things God will do
  c) things God has done.

3 Choose three beliefs which you think might particularly affect the life of a Jewish believer. Explain your choice and describe how these might affect a believer's life.

4 If you have already studied another religion in your course, say whether followers of that religion would agree or disagree with each statement in Source A.

SAVE AS...

5 Add to your copy of the chart above a final row summarising Jewish beliefs about God. Use Source A to help you.

Thirteen Principles of Faith

In the twelfth century the Jewish scholar Maimonides in his thirteen Principles of Faith tried to sum up Jewish beliefs. These are the beliefs that he felt were essential to Judaism and distinguished Judaism from other faiths. (See page 98 for more about Maimonides.)

A

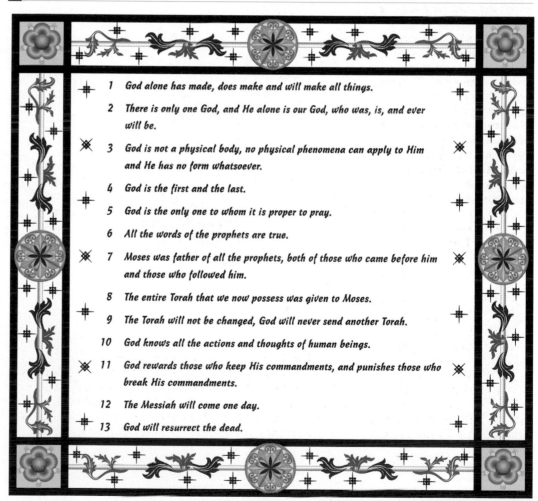

1 God alone has made, does make and will make all things.

2 There is only one God, and He alone is our God, who was, is, and ever will be.

3 God is not a physical body, no physical phenomena can apply to Him and He has no form whatsoever.

4 God is the first and the last.

5 God is the only one to whom it is proper to pray.

6 All the words of the prophets are true.

7 Moses was father of all the prophets, both of those who came before him and those who followed him.

8 The entire Torah that we now possess was given to Moses.

9 The Torah will not be changed, God will never send another Torah.

10 God knows all the actions and thoughts of human beings.

11 God rewards those who keep His commandments, and punishes those who break His commandments.

12 The Messiah will come one day.

13 God will resurrect the dead.

Maimonides' thirteen Principles of Faith. A poetic version is sung as part of synagogue services.

1.4 Ways of being Jewish in Britain today

Diversity of Jewish traditions

Source A makes the divisions between the different groups appear fixed.

However, as is often the case with religion, things are not as simple as they seem. Religion is dynamic – constantly changing. Jews are individual human beings who consider things from their own point of view. They seek personal guidance from God. They follow their own conscience. Some Jews are very sure of God. Some go through periods of doubt. Most find that their beliefs and practices change over time. Some Jews move from one tradition to another, combining elements of each.

Each band in the chart embraces many Jews. They may observe the same rituals, but hold varying beliefs.

The chart shows only Jews in Britain. In other countries the balance is different.

So, avoid generalisations when you answer questions about Judaism.

- Avoid saying 'Jews believe...', since this chart and this book will make clear to you that there is a wide range of beliefs within Judaism. Instead write 'Some Jews...' or name the specific tradition. Remember that in your exam you will have to show you are aware of more than one tradition.
- Equally important, remember that *within* each tradition there is diversity of practice and belief. Use words like 'many' and 'some' to show that you recognise this.

Source A shows the main Jewish traditions in Britain today. In this book we will focus on the Orthodox and Reform traditions in particular. Most case studies will come from members either of the United Synagogue (Orthodox) or of the Reform Synagogue.

A

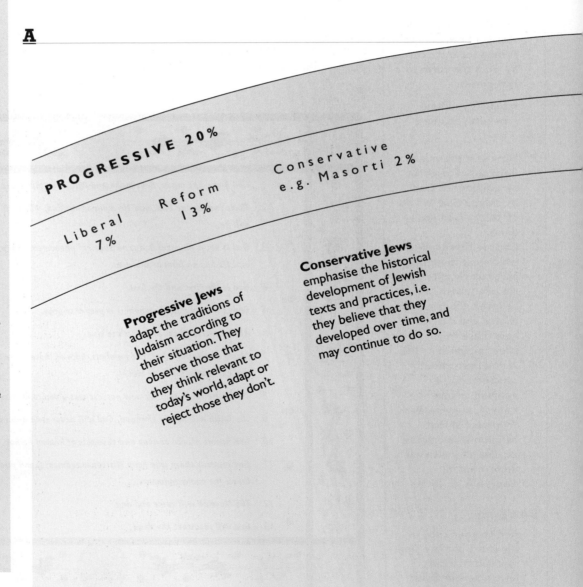

PROGRESSIVE 20%

Liberal 7%

Reform 13%

Conservative e.g. Masorti 2%

Progressive Jews adapt the traditions of Judaism according to their situation. They observe those that they think relevant to today's world, adapt or reject those they don't.

Conservative Jews emphasise the historical development of Jewish texts and practices, i.e. they believe that they developed over time, and may continue to do so.

> It is said that if there are two Jews on a desert island, they will set up three synagogues!

1 **This joke, told by Jews, says something about how they see themselves. What impression does it give you of the diversity within Judaism?**

B

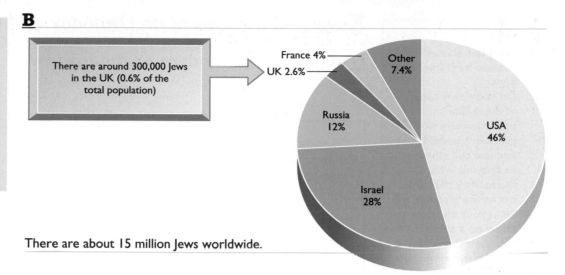

There are around 300,000 Jews in the UK (0.6% of the total population)

France 4%
UK 2.6%
Other 7.4%
Russia 12%
USA 46%
Israel 28%

There are about 15 million Jews worldwide.

ORTHODOX 70–80%

Over 50% of Orthodox Jews are members of the United Synagogue

ULTRA-ORTHODOX 6%

Chasidic Jews e.g. Lubavitch

Orthodox Jews follow the traditional practices of Judaism. They believe the Torah was given complete by God to Moses on Mount Sinai and observe the laws and traditions of Judaism. They do not have female rabbis.

Ultra-Orthodox Jews make few compromises with the modern world. For example, they wear traditional dress and they do not have televisions in their homes. This is the fastest-growing sector of Judaism.

Each band embraces Jews with a wide range of personal beliefs. The practices might look similar but the beliefs will vary greatly. For example, while Orthodox Jews might share common practices when they worship or meet together, they may hold different beliefs about these things from others they are worshipping with.

Secular Jews

Judaism is the religion of the Jewish people, not all of whom are observant or 'religious'. Many non-religious Jews have a strong sense of ethnic identity. Anyone with a Jewish mother is regarded as a Jew. So, in addition to the 'practising' Jews, there are SECULAR, or ethnic, Jews. They might have a strong sense of shared identity with practising Jews, aware that they share a common history, but be ATHEISTS or AGNOSTICS themselves. They might call themselves Jews, yet not hold any of the beliefs associated with Judaism or observe the practices of the Jewish traditions shown in the chart.

A week in the lives of an Orthodox and a Reform Jew

Daniel Rose – a modern Orthodox Jew

C

Monday

The school day starts with prayers. After last night's wedding party and dancing, I nearly missed Shacharit (see Activity question 2), but at least I was there and I don't think any of my students noticed.

I joined my family to light the menorah for the second day of Chanukah. My family bought me some new CDs – that should help me keep up-to-date with the kids at school.

Tuesday

Meeting about Year 12 trip to Poland next year. I am taking them to meet the Jewish communities there and to visit the site of a concentration camp.

I have mixed feelings about the trip. We must remember the Shoah, but there is so much to be positive and proud about in being Jewish that we shouldn't focus only on our tragic past. At least we should use these memories to strengthen our feelings of 'peoplehood', as well as to say to the world that we will never allow this to happen again – not to us, or to any people.

Wednesday

I had my Torah study session early so I could go to the Arsenal match tonight. This keeps me going spiritually the rest of the week. And Arsenal won two nil! Good day!

Thursday

I went to a great shiur by a very inspiring rabbi. It was a study of the reading for next Shabbat. I think it is important to keep up with my own personal learning, however busy I am.

Friday

It's winter, so school finished at 1 p.m. to get ready for Shabbat. After the Friday night service, a short one with some beautiful tunes, dinner with the whole family – grandparents and all. A real rest – no work, no travelling, no TV; just catch up on everyone's news for the week.

Shabbat

On Shabbat morning my cousin had his Bar Mitzvah in shul. He read the Torah really well. A great moment, which we'll celebrate with a party tomorrow night.

After sunset, Shabbat over, another party – this time a farewell. Friends are making Aliya, which means they are going to live in Israel (literally 'going up'). I intend to live in Israel too, one day. I told them that they have about a year to find me a house, a wife and a job. It was a great party, with loads of their friends and family there to wish them well.

Daniel Rose teaches Jewish Studies at Immanuel College (a Jewish independent secondary school) in Bushey, Hertfordshire.

Sara Anton – a modern Reform Jew

D

Sunday

I taught cheder this morning, so no lie-in. The class was really good; we sat outside and had a chat about the Shoah and what it means to them. It was interesting to hear how aware of it they are, and also how little anti-Semitism they have all experienced.

I wonder how much the Shoah has affected my generation – I think about it a lot and find it hard to understand how such a thing could have happened. I know it binds me to my Judaism even more closely.

Monday

Today was an amazing day; I went to my first brit – my twin nephews'. As I watched the mohel I was aware that Jews have been carrying out this ritual for thousands of years. I felt the connection that I and now my nephews have to this rich culture. But at the same time I struggle with some aspects of Judaism, especially the sexism that I see.

Wednesday

I met up with close friends this evening. They're all Jewish. I met them when I spent a year at university in Jerusalem. Sometimes I find it hard living in England, especially because of the pressure to marry someone Jewish. In many ways I feel very English – this is where I grew up – but I celebrate all the Jewish festivals, go to synagogue on Shabbat, and most of my friends are Jewish.

Thursday

Started planning my holiday to Israel to stay with my best friend. In many ways it feels like home. I love the fact that the national holidays are Jewish festivals, and food in shops and restaurants and supermarkets is kosher. Many Reform Jews don't keep kosher, but I think of it as a constant reminder that I'm Jewish. Also, it's a difficult thing to do, and I like to know that I can be disciplined at least in one area of my life!

Friday

I really enjoyed going to synagogue tonight, such a beautiful service. Afterwards I went home and had a meal with my parents. Mum is the world's best cook – she calls her chicken soup 'Jewish penicillin'. It's so good to take time to eat a good meal, talk about the week and be with my family.

Judaism is like a heartbeat to me, but it's not always easy to live with. I remember my friends at school would go to parties on a Friday night, and I couldn't because my family stayed in and ate together. I love lighting the candles with my mother and having a family meal, but nonetheless, it was often hard to be different.

Saturday

I don't keep Shabbat in an Orthodox way – I drive, write and switch on lights, but I try to make something about the day restful and special. Today I went to synagogue and then to a friend for lunch and a walk. It was good to stop running around after such a frantic week.

Sara Anton is a teacher who has worked in England and Israel.

1.5   How do Jews make moral decisions?

Sources of moral authority
The Jews have been called
'The People of the Book'.
In Judaism, written sacred texts
are very important. The
greatest sources of authority
for practising Jews today are
the Torah and the TALMUD.
Diagram A shows how the
Torah, the Talmud and other
Jewish sacred texts were
created and have been passed
down to Jews today.

Units 2–4 of this book are about morality. Morality is the study of right and wrong.
You are now going to think about how Jews make moral decisions.

A

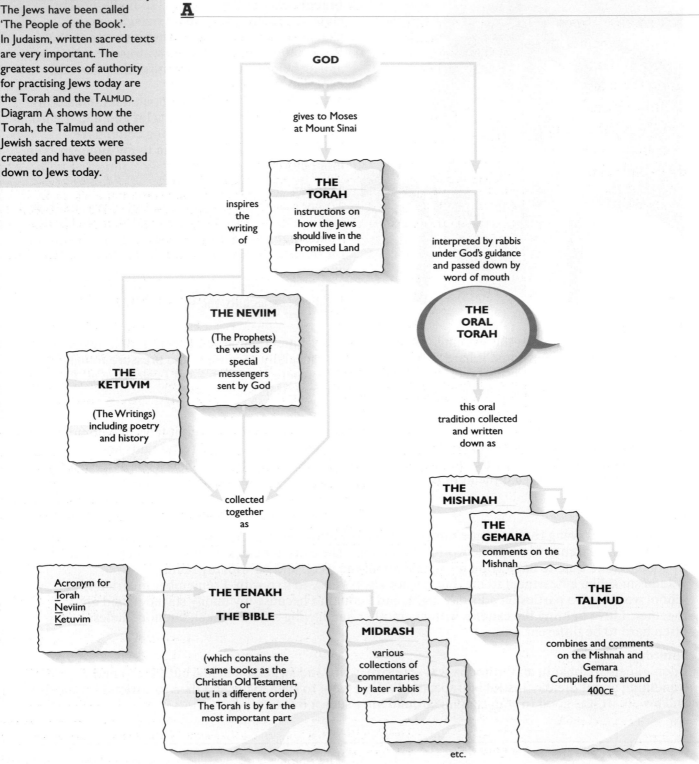

GOD

gives to Moses
at Mount Sinai

**THE
TORAH**

instructions on
how the Jews
should live in the
Promised Land

inspires
the
writing
of

interpreted by rabbis
under God's guidance
and passed down by
word of mouth

**THE
ORAL
TORAH**

THE NEVIIM

(The Prophets)
the words of
special
messengers
sent by God

**THE
KETUVIM**

(The Writings)
including poetry
and history

this oral
tradition collected
and written
down as

**THE
MISHNAH**

**THE
GEMARA**

comments on the
Mishnah

collected
together
as

Acronym for
Torah
Neviim
Ketuvim

**THE TENAKH
or
THE BIBLE**

(which contains the
same books as the
Christian Old Testament,
but in a different order)
The Torah is by far the
most important part

MIDRASH

various
collections of
commentaries
by later rabbis

**THE
TALMUD**

combines and comments
on the Mishnah and
Gemara
Compiled from around
400CE

etc.

How do these sources of authority relate to one another?

To see how Jews use these sources of authority, and how the different sources work together, it is best to consider an example. Let's take the example of Shabbat (the Sabbath) which is a special day, set aside to honour God.

The Torah is always the starting point. This gives the big ideas. The later Jewish writings consist of debate and discussion about those big ideas.

Source of authority	What it says about Shabbat
The Torah This consists of the first five books of the Bible and lays the foundations. It gives the big ideas.	The fourth of the Ten Commandments (Exodus 20.4) is the instruction to keep the Sabbath day holy. This is the big idea! But what does this mean in practice? The main guidance is not to work. Just as God rested from Creation on the seventh day so must you. You honour God by not working on the Sabbath. Exodus 35 contains one very specific instruction: not to 'kindle a flame' (light a fire) on the Shabbat – but that's about it. Of course, people wanted to know what else counts as work and what doesn't. Enter the Mishnah.
The Mishnah This records the teaching of the written Torah, but teases it out in more detail.	The MISHNAH lists 39 categories of work that are forbidden on Shabbat. It spells out teaching about them in some detail. It also adds some guidance on 'kindling a flame'. For example, it explains that on Shabbat even kindling a flame to burn spices in the Tabernacle (the tent used before the Temple was built) is prohibited.
The Gemara This is an extended commentary on the Mishnah from the second century CE. The Mishnah and the Gemara together form the main body of the **Talmud**. This is more important to Jews than the later stages.	The GEMARA probes further to apply these teachings to every conceivable situation at that time. Are there exceptions to the rule about not lighting a fire? For example, can you light a fire to heat water to help a sick person? The answer in the Talmud is yes. 'We warm water for him right away, because wherever there is doubt as to whether a life may be in danger, the laws of the Shabbat may be suspended.' But at the same time the Talmud underlines that you cannot light a fire to bake bread on Shabbat, nor do any cooking.
The Shulchan Aruch Code of Jewish law	This sixteenth-century code of Jewish law simplified the ordering of the Talmud and added practical advice. For example, if you can't cook on the Sabbath when should you cook? The Shulchan Aruch gives guidance on how to prepare hot food and drink for Shabbat.
Rabbinic Responsa Contemporary law	This process is ongoing. New questions arise: • with the invention of the car – is it permitted to drive on Shabbat? It is not, since driving a car counts as lighting a fire (the spark that fires the petrol). • with the invention of electricity – is switching on a light on Shabbat allowed? Again, no, since this is creating a spark. However, lights can be left on throughout the Shabbat, or can come on in response to a pre-set timer.

This results in many different opinions. In any one case it is up to the individual or the group, e.g. the synagogue, to decide what feels right for them.

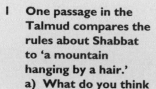

I One passage in the Talmud compares the rules about Shabbat to 'a mountain hanging by a hair.'
a) What do you think this means?
b) Do you agree?

The Talmud

Judaism recognises that it is hard to apply even simple rules to complex modern problems. The Talmud is therefore concerned with debate and discussion. As you can see from Source B, each page of the Talmud contains an extract of Mishnah and layers of discussion and debate on the extract. So reading the Talmud is like listening to a conversation in which different rabbis give their views. Sometimes the problem is left unresolved and it is up to later generations to join in the debate and reach their own conclusions.

B

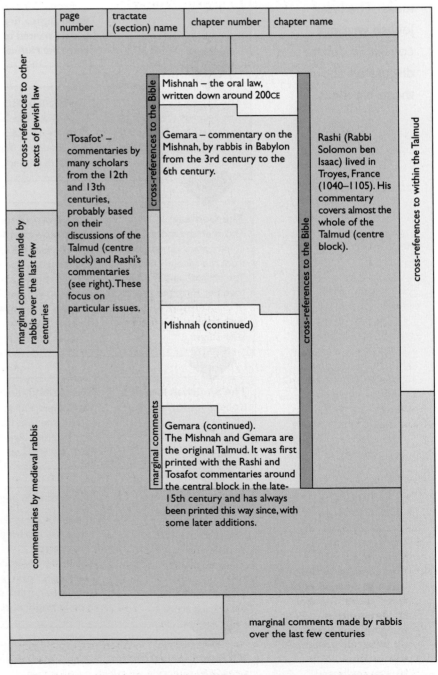

| page number | tractate (section) name | chapter number | chapter name |

cross-references to other texts of Jewish law

cross-references to the Bible

Mishnah – the oral law, written down around 200CE

Gemara – commentary on the Mishnah, by rabbis in Babylon from the 3rd century to the 6th century.

'Tosafot' – commentaries by many scholars from the 12th and 13th centuries, probably based on their discussions of the Talmud (centre block) and Rashi's commentaries (see right). These focus on particular issues.

Rashi (Rabbi Solomon ben Isaac) lived in Troyes, France (1040–1105). His commentary covers almost the whole of the Talmud (centre block).

cross-references to within the Talmud

marginal comments made by rabbis over the last few centuries

Mishnah (continued)

cross-references to the Bible

marginal comments

Gemara (continued). The Mishnah and Gemara are the original Talmud. It was first printed with the Rashi and Tosafot commentaries around the central block in the late-15th century and has always been printed this way since, with some later additions.

commentaries by medieval rabbis

marginal comments made by rabbis over the last few centuries

A page of Talmud, together with a 'map' of the page

SAVE AS...

At a couple of points through this book, you might be able to use the sources you are given to create your own page of debate a bit like a page of Talmud. Practise this by recording the ideas in the table on the previous page as if it was a page of Talmud.

On the right you can see how the page of Talmud above has been built up. The various parts are linked in a similar way to items on an Internet site. In fact, if you go to the website at http://www.ucalgary.ca/~elsegal/TalmudPage.html and click on each section in turn you can find out more about how the Talmud developed, and read translations of the text on this Talmud page.

Orthodox and Reform attitudes to the Torah

One of the main distinctions between the Orthodox and Reform traditions is in their attitude to the Torah.

Orthodox

> Orthodox Jews believe that the Torah is God-given and timeless and that the mitzvot in the Torah are as relevant today as when they were given to Moses. Orthodox Jews look to the principles of the Torah for guidance to deal with the changing circumstances of the modern world. God wants Jews to keep the commandments of the Torah. We do our utmost to follow the Torah in every detail and would not set its teachings aside.

Reform

> Reform Jews believe that the Torah is the central revelation from God, but not that it was handed down in a finished form to Moses on Mount Sinai. We view it as a human document. Over the thousands of years since the Torah was given, there have been further revelations from God. The Torah must be reinterpreted in the light of developments in society to ensure that it remains relevant. Reform Jews feel free to set aside the teaching of the Torah if it is not relevant to modern life.

✓ CHECKPOINT

You will need to know the meaning of these two terms:

- ABSOLUTE MORALITY — this is when a person believes that there is a right course of action in a moral dilemma that is true in all situations, regardless of culture, religious tradition, time or age. For example: 'it is always wrong to kill.'

  There are few moral issues on which Jews are likely to take an absolutist approach. Among the exceptions are idol-worship and adultery, which are never acceptable to Jews.

- RELATIVE MORALITY — this is when a person has strong beliefs or principles but they believe that different courses of action might be needed in different situations. For example: 'it is usually wrong to kill, but sometimes it might be necessary for a particular reason.'

  Jews are likely to take a relativist approach to moral decisions. They are likely to say that the Torah gives principles that Jews can apply differently to different situations.

Through the rest of this book you will be coming across many examples of the different ways in which Orthodox and Reform traditions apply the principles of Judaism to modern day-to-day situations and ethical issues.

ACTIVITY

No individual could remember or understand all Jewish teaching. The Talmud tells a story about a man who challenged Hillel, a rabbi in the first century CE, to teach him the whole of the Torah while he stood on one leg. His answer is in the cartoon opposite.

  His answer is a version of what has become known as the Golden Rule. It has been adopted by many non-religious people as well as by various religions as the simplest guide to moral behaviour and decision-making.

See if you can learn Rabbi Hillel's Golden Rule off by heart while standing on one leg (it will be very useful in your exam!).

How long can you stand on one leg?

Not for long!

Well then... Love your neighbour as yourself. That is the whole of the Torah. The rest is simply comment on it. Go away and study.

The Moral Ocean

How do you decide between right and wrong?

- Do you ask advice from other people?
- Do you think of what your religion or upbringing has taught you?
- Do you work out an answer for yourself?
- Do you think, 'What would happen if . . .' and go for the option with the best outcome?
- Do you think, 'What would so-and-so do in this situation?' and try to follow their example?
- Do you have a different way altogether?

Making moral decisions is a little like steering a ship through dangerous or exciting unknown waters. To help you reach a decision with which you are happy and that you feel is right there are islands you can visit. These islands are your sources of moral authority.

This illustration shows some of the sources of moral authority which might guide a Jewish person.

WHAT SHALL I DO?

Conscience

Internet

Secular wisdom

TV

Talmud

Torah

DECISION I SHOULD MAKE

Rabbi

FOCUS TASK

1   Work with a partner.
    On your own copy of the Moral Ocean diagram plot the route that might be taken by
    a Jewish person. They can visit only five islands. Make sure they visit their most
    important island first. If you think that there might be differences between the routes
    taken by an Orthodox Jew, such as Daniel Rose (see page 14), and a Reform Jew, such
    as Sara Anton (see page 15), use two different colours to mark the routes.
2   What differences, if any, are there between a Jew's route and the route you might
    take? You may want to label the empty island. Add more if you need to.

SAVE AS . . .

3   What does the Jewish route say about the way Jews make moral decisions? Use the
    structure below to write four paragraphs to explain the Jewish route across the Moral
    Ocean diagram. You will need to refer to pages 16–19.

    • Sources of authority are . . .
    • The main sources of authority for Jews are . . .
    • The first island a Jew might visit . . .
    • Jews might also visit . . .

Review tasks

A

Behind the rules and principles of Judaism lie a set of values. The rules are an expression of a set of values. A value is a conviction about what is important in life.

Here is a list of things that people often value highly.

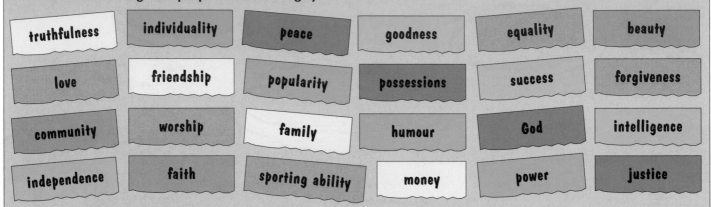

truthfulness   individuality   peace   goodness   equality   beauty

love   friendship   popularity   possessions   success   forgiveness

community   worship   family   humour   God   intelligence

independence   faith   sporting ability   money   power   justice

1 Choose the four items that you most value.
   For each item you have chosen, complete the following sentence:
   I value ... because...
2 From what you have so far learned about Judaism choose four items that you think are particularly valued in Judaism. They might be the same four as you chose above, or they might not. You may want to add a value that is not listed above. For each one, complete the following sentence:
   I think Jews value ... because...
   Keep your sentences. Later in the course you will look back to them to see if you want to change or add anything.

B

In the modern world, religion is not the only approach to making moral decisions:

1 Look at the diagram on the right. Use a dictionary to look up any words you do not understand. Match each type of principle in the diagram to a definition and to an explanation from the lists below.

Definitions
- **Considers the overall good of humanity**
- **Considers the law of the land**
- **Considers God**
- **Considers personal pleasure**

Explanations
- **Whatever pleases God is right. Whatever displeases God is wrong.**
- **Whatever is legal is right. Whatever is illegal is wrong.**
- **Whatever gives me pleasure is right. Whatever gives me pain is wrong.**
- **Whatever brings the most good to the most people is right. Whatever harms many people is wrong.**

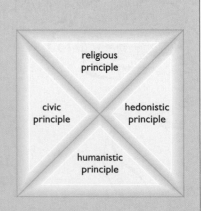

religious principle

civic principle   hedonistic principle

humanistic principle

2 Which approach would you say best describes *your* guiding principle?
3 Which approach would you say best describes the guiding principle of Judaism?
4 Write a paragraph explaining the difference between something being legal and it being morally acceptable to a religious believer.

UNIT 2

Issues of life and death

I call heaven and earth to witness
against you this day: I have put before
you life and death, blessing and curse.

CHOOSE LIFE

– if you and your offspring
would live – by loving the Lord your God,
heeding His commands, and holding fast
to Him. For thereby you shall have life and
shall long endure upon the soil that the Lord
your God swore to your ancestors, Abraham,
Isaac, and Jacob, to give to them.

Deuteronomy 30.19–20

Jews believe that God is the source of all life. But in today's society human beings
have greater power over life and death than ever before. There are more
opportunities for ordinary people to make choices about life and death. For
example, 40 years ago abortion was illegal in Britain. Now it is legal. A decision
which used to be taken for you is now left to the individual. Jews would say that
making something legal does not necessarily make it morally acceptable.

In this unit you are going to see some of the different ways in which their faith
can guide Jews in making moral decisions about life and death. You are also
going to make up your own mind about how far Jewish ideas can help non-Jews
make moral decisions.

2.1　The sanctity of life

In considering issues of life and death, the Jewish belief in the SANCTITY OF LIFE is the most important belief to bear in mind. What does this mean?

God is the source of life
Humans are made 'in the image of God'. This does not mean that they look like God, but that God puts something special into humans, sometimes called the 'soul'. This means that human beings have the potential to do good and to seek out God.

Life is sacred and should be preserved at all costs
Life is so important that even the laws of Shabbat may be broken in order to save a life.

Every life has a purpose
Every child is born to develop spiritually. Each Jew therefore has a God-given purpose – to live as God wishes through learning Torah and doing mitzvot. Even someone whose quality of life is diminished by illness has this to aim for in their life.

God decides when someone's life should end
No human has the right to do this. The only reasons in Jewish law for cutting short a life are if a person is forced to kill someone in self-defence or in a war, or as a punishment in rare cases set out in the Torah.

These are simple and powerful ideas. But how do Jews apply them to everyday life? Do they mean that Jews are always against abortion in all cases, or always opposed to euthanasia and capital punishment? What do you think?
Read on and find out if you are right.

A

You shall not murder.

Exodus 20.13. The sixth of the Ten Commandments

B

You made all the delicate, inner parts of my body and knitted them together in my mother's womb . . . You were there while I was being formed in utter seclusion. You saw me before I was born and scheduled each day of my life before I began to breathe. Each day was recorded in your book.

Psalm 139.13–16 (from the *Good News Bible*)

C

The Torah tells us that men and women were created in God's image and we do not own our own body. We are proprietors of bodies that were given to us in safekeeping until such time as God decides to revoke our lives.

Dr Lisa Aiken, an American Orthodox Jew and author of *To be a Jewish Woman*

D

In whatever body and whatever disabled mind, there is a soul cast in the image of God.

Dr Jonathan Sacks is Chief Rabbi of the United Synagogue (Orthodox), the biggest Jewish organisation in Great Britain.

SAVE AS...

1 On a piece of paper no bigger than a postcard sum up the teachings of Judaism about the sanctity of life. Choose just one of Sources A–D to include in your summary. Which one do you feel best sums up Jewish ideas about the sanctity of life?

DISCUSS

2 How do you think the story in Source F might affect Jewish attitudes to:
   a) medical research to help childless couples
   b) abortion?

Children are a blessing from God

In Jewish tradition having children is both a privilege and a duty. God's intention was for people 'to multiply.' Barrenness (an old term for being unable to have children) was seen as a curse; having children a blessing. Throughout the TENAKH God intervenes to help those who are childless. Prophets, priests, and rabbis have always given their blessing to childless couples hoping that this will change their situation.

One of the most celebrated modern doctors who has helped thousands of childless couples to have their own children is Robert Winston. He is an Orthodox Jew. In Source E he explains his motivation.

E

> It is entirely natural that I as a Jew should be involved in this work: helping the childless to conceive. It is so much part of our Jewish heritage that childlessness is an unhappiness, even a curse. The suffering of women in the Bible, such as Sarah or Hannah (see Source F), when they cry out to God for a child is painful and moving...

Professor Robert Winston with pictures of some of the babies whose conception was assisted by him and his team

F

Elkanah ... had two wives, one named Hannah ... but Hannah was childless ... for the Lord had closed her womb. [The other wife], to make her miserable, would taunt her that the Lord had closed her womb. This happened year after year.

... In her wretchedness [Hannah] prayed to the Lord, weeping all the while. And she made this vow: 'O Lord of Hosts, if You will look upon the suffering of Your maidservant and will remember me ... and if You will grant Your maidservant a male child, I will dedicate him to the Lord for all the days of his life ...'

As she kept on praying before the Lord, Eli (the priest) watched her ... [Hannah said,] 'I am a very unhappy woman ... I have been pouring out my heart to the Lord ... I have ... been speaking all this time out of my great anguish and distress.' 'Then go in peace,' said Eli, 'and may the God of Israel grant you what you have asked of Him.' ...

... the Lord remembered her. Hannah conceived, and at the turn of the year bore a son. She named him Samuel, meaning, 'I asked the Lord for him.' ... And Hannah prayed:

> *My heart exults in the Lord;*
> *I have triumphed through the Lord.*
> *I gloat over my enemies;*
> *I rejoice in your deliverance ...*

I Samuel 1.1–2.1

How do Jews deal with death?

Judaism is strongly rooted in this life. Jews are encouraged to focus on practical ethical behaviour now, rather than concentrate on rewards in the life to come. However, an awareness of death can help Jews to approach life with an appropriate attitude.

After someone in their family dies, Judaism provides precise burial and mourning rituals. These help Jews to express their grief. They also help the Jewish community to support the bereaved. These rituals are summarised in Source I.

1 Read Sources G and H. Choose one and explain:
a) the speaker's attitude to death
b) how you think this attitude might affect their actions in life
c) whether you think it is a good attitude to take. Give your reasons.

G

Everyone must have two pockets, so that he can reach into the one or the other, according to his needs. In his right pocket are to be the words, 'For my sake was the world created,' and in the left, 'I am dust and ashes.'

Rabbi Bunam of Pzhysha who died in 1827

H

A story is told about the tourist who came to visit the Chafetz Chayim, one of the wise rabbis of eastern Europe. The tourist surveyed the rabbi's room and saw only a table, a chair, a cupboard, a bookcase, and a bed.
'Where are your possessions?' he asked.
*'Where are **your** possessions?' replied the rabbi.*
'What do you mean, "Where are my possessions?"' asked the tourist. 'I am just a visitor here.'
'So am I,' said the Chafetz Chayim.

I

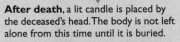

Before someone dies he or she says the opening words of the Shema (see page 1).

After death, a lit candle is placed by the deceased's head. The body is not left alone from this time until it is buried.

Members of the CHEVRA KADISHA (the burial society) wash the body in a ritual way. They wrap it in a simple white linen sheet – rich and poor are equal in death – and, for a man, place his TALLIT (prayer shawl) around his shoulders. They will often share the role of staying with the body, reading Psalms and other appropriate prayers, and speaking respectfully of the deceased.

The immediate mourners (parents, siblings, children, spouse) make a small tear in their clothes to show their sadness.

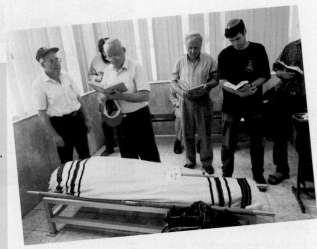

The funeral follows as soon as possible after the death, usually the next day. The body is placed in a simple biodegradable wooden coffin with rope handles to show that nothing material lasts.

After a short service the body is taken on a simple wooden cart to a cemetery. In Hebrew the cemetery is called either BET OLAM, which means 'House of eternity', or BET CHAYIM, which means 'House of life'.

After a few words from the rabbi, the coffin is lowered into the ground. The closest relative then shovels the first soil into the grave and reads the KADDISH. This is a prayer praising God and asking God for peace and life on Earth.

Cremation is never practised by Orthodox Jews – this reflects the belief that people may need their bodies in the afterlife and that the body belongs to God, so people may not destroy it. However, some Reform Jews believe that the soul lives on but the body is not needed. They therefore find cremation acceptable.

2 Why do you think Jews light memorial candles?

3 Who would you want to light a candle for? Why?

ACTIVITY

I With a partner, make a list of all the Jewish rituals surrounding death. Sort them into the following categories:

• to show respect
• to preserve the memory
• to prepare for life after death
• other.

SAVE AS...

2 Write two paragraphs to explain:
   a) which of these rituals you think *you* might find helpful if you were mourning
   b) which you might not find helpful.
   Give your reasons.

On each anniversary of the death and on YOM KIPPUR (the Day of Atonement) mourners light a YARZHEIT candle, which burns for 24 hours, and say Kaddish.

Before lighting the candle the person prays: *Today I remember with love (name) who has gone to everlasting life, and I honour his/her memory. As this light burns pure and clear, so may the thought of his/her goodness shine in my heart and strengthen me, Lord, to do your will. Amen.*

As they light the candle they say: *The memory of the righteous is as a blessing.*

Jews also light Yarzheit candles on YOM HASHOAH (Holocaust memorial day), in memory of all those who died in the Holocaust.

If practical, mourners may **visit the grave** often. Each time, they lay a small pebble on the grave. This tradition was established by Abraham, who laid a stone on the grave of his wife Sarah to show where she was buried.

For 30 days, the mourners do not cut their hair or attend parties. Men don't shave.

The Kaddish is recited each day for eleven months after death.

For twelve months people mourning a parent or a child try not to attend joyful events.

Then follows the ritual of SHIVA. For seven days the mourners spend their waking hours at the home of any one mourner, sitting on low seats and comforting each other. This is an opportunity for relatives and friends to visit and comfort the mourners by speaking about the deceased, sharing memories and anecdotes. The three daily prayer services are said at the shiva house.

Life after death?

Jews have different ideas about what happens after death. Many Jews say that it is a mystery. It is believed that the soul lives on after death. According to Maimonides, the resurrection of the dead is one of the thirteen Principles of Faith for Jews (see page 11): when the Messiah comes the bodies of those who have died will be raised to life again.

After death a series of rituals support the mourners and ensure that the memory of the deceased lives on.

2.2 Do Jews agree about abortion?

Rachel is seventeen, pregnant and confused. She never meant to get pregnant. Before this happened she was planning to go to university next year. A baby would make that impossible.

She lives in Britain and legally she could have an abortion, but she is also a practising Jew, and she doesn't want to go against the teachings of her religion. It is too late to say she should not have got pregnant in the first place; that's in the past. But now she wants to do the right thing. Sources A–E represent some of the Jewish voices she might hear . . .

A

When the Master of Creation determines that life should begin we have no right to decide that we know better than He about how and when to end it.

Judaism does not view abortion as a solution for people who wish to be sexually active without accepting responsibility for the consequences.

Dr Lisa Aiken, an American Orthodox Jew and author of *To be a Jewish Woman*

B

I don't personally have a problem with the idea of a Jewish woman having an abortion. I see the embryo in its early stages as being a promise of life rather than alive, since it is not yet a separate conscious being.

Judith Green is a member of a Reform synagogue in North London. She sees her views as more radical than most.

D

Abortion is allowed . . . where facilities are available for it to be carried out legally and safely . . . The right of an adult woman to make decisions about her own life has to be considered.

Rabbi Jonathan Romain in *Faith and Practice: a Guide to Reform Judaism*

C

Jewish people today live in the shadow of the Holocaust. One and a half million Jewish children were murdered by the Nazis. Today many Jews feel strongly that it is their responsibility to play their part to ensure the continuity of the Jewish people. This, plus a deep-seated belief that life is sacred, makes abortion a difficult choice for a Jewish woman.

Barbara Joseph is a Reform Jew.

E

If a woman is having a very difficult labour, then the embryo may be dismembered inside her and removed limb by limb, because her life takes precedence over its life. If most of the embryo has emerged [from its mother] however, then we may not touch it, since we are not allowed to give precedence to one life over another life.

Mishnah Oholot 7.6 – the earliest reference to abortion. This refers to abortion during labour. At this time (the second century) surgical skills were very basic. Abortion would only be possible at this very late stage.

DISCUSS

1 Study Sources A–E. Which speakers condemn abortion? Which allow abortion?
2 What arguments for or against abortion are offered by these sources?
3 Is it possible from this evidence to say whether it would be acceptable to Jews for Rachel to have an abortion?
4 In *your* view, would it be acceptable for Rachel to have an abortion? Does anyone in your class think abortion is:
   a) always wrong
   b) never wrong?
5 What do you think have been the most important factors influencing your viewpoint on abortion?

Why do Jews disagree about abortion?

The Torah is the Jews' greatest source of authority. However, it does not have anything specific to say about abortion. So (as is so often the case with ethical issues) Jewish teachers need to go back to first principles and apply them to the issue of abortion.

✓ CHECKPOINT

Abortion in Britain

Before 1968 abortion was illegal in Britain. Since the 1968 Abortion Act abortion has been legal in Britain if:

- two doctors agree that it is needed
- it is carried out on registered premises
- the baby is not yet capable of surviving. (The legal term used is 'viable' – this means 'able to survive apart from the mother if born and cared for medically'.)

In deciding if an abortion is needed, doctors must consider whether:

- the life, physical health or mental health of the mother is at risk
- an existing family will suffer if the pregnancy continues
- there is a reasonable chance that the child will be born handicapped.

In 1968 the latest termination date in cases of risk to the mother's mental health or an existing family was set at 28 weeks, reduced in 1990 to 24 weeks. There is now no time limit in cases of risk to the mother's life or health or of the baby being handicapped.

The number of abortions has risen steadily.

In practice 'the mental health of the mother' has been interpreted to include distress of the mother regarding pregnancy or motherhood. Some people say that Britain effectively has 'abortion on demand'. Some would even say that abortion is now treated as a form of contraception.

The law allows medical staff to abstain from performing abortions. However, some who have tried to opt out have found their jobs at risk.

The main principle affecting Jewish teaching is that life is a gift from God. Life is holy or sacred (see page 24). Even an embryo has life, so abortion is murder.

However, the mother's life is also sacred. What if the mother will die if the pregnancy continues? Most Jews (Orthodox and Reform) would agree that if they had to choose then the mother's life takes precedence (see Source E). In fact, most would argue that if the mother's life is at risk then an abortion *should* be done.

But what if the mother's life is not at risk, but simply her happiness, or her quality of life? Now we hit the areas of disagreement. For Reform Jews and some, but by no means all, Orthodox Jews, the risk to the mother's life extends to the risk of mental illness, suicide, homicidal (murderous) behaviour or emotional stress or breakdown caused by pregnancy. Some Reform Jews even believe that poverty is grounds for an abortion, but Orthodox Jews strongly disagree.

There was bitter debate between Orthodox and Reform leaders when an abortion law was passed in Israel in 1977. Both Orthodox and Reform agreed that abortion should be allowed when the mother's life is in danger, but . . .

Reform
Reform leaders in Israel argued for (and got) a law that also allows abortion:

- when the mother is under sixteen
- when the pregnancy results from rape or incest
- when a baby would be born with severe mental or physical handicap.

Orthodox
Abortion for any other reason was fiercely opposed by Orthodox Jews. The Reform view won. But some Orthodox rabbis still do not accept abortion in cases of rape or when the fetus is abnormal, even where the law of the land allows it.

FOCUS TASK

1 **What do you think**
   a) **an Orthodox rabbi**
   b) **a Reform rabbi**
   would advise Rachel to do?
2 **Explain why it is possible for Orthodox and Reform Jews to disagree about abortion even though they both start from the Torah. You may wish to refer back to page 19.**
3 **Abortion used to be illegal in Britain. Now it is legal. A decision that used to be taken for you is now left to the individual's conscience. Do you think this is a good thing or a bad thing? Explain your view carefully, showing that you have considered another point of view.**

2.3 How do Jews respond to terminal illness?

The British Social Attitudes Survey asked thousands of people their views on euthanasia in a variety of situations. Source A shows the scenarios they considered.

A

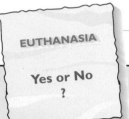

EUTHANASIA

Yes or No
?

SCENARIOS

A

has a terminal and painful form of cancer and has probably got six months to live.

B

has a terminal illness but is not in pain. B has probably got some years to live.

C

is not in pain or in danger of death, but has become permanently and completely dependent on relatives who find it a burden caring for them.

D

is not ill, or close to death, but is lonely and depressed and wishes to die and has told many people so.

E

has a terminal illness, and is on a life-support system – they will die if it is switched off – and is thought to be too ill to make their own decisions.

F

has incurable and painful arthritis which is severely limiting their quality of life, but will not die from it.

G

is in a coma, never expected to regain consciousness, but is not on a life-support system.

✓ CHECKPOINT

What is euthanasia?
Euthanasia is the term used to describe ending a person's life deliberately, but for compassionate reasons. The term means 'gentle and easy death'.

Euthanasia in Britain
Euthanasia is illegal in Britain. There have been a number of attempts to get a bill through Parliament legalising euthanasia. All have failed. One example was a bill in 1969. If it had been passed, it would have allowed euthanasia on request to anyone over eighteen, provided that 'two doctors believed the patient to be suffering from a serious physical illness or impairment, reasonably thought to be incurable, and expected to cause considerable distress.'

VOLUNTARY EUTHANASIA is when a person asks for their own life to be ended.

COMPULSORY or INVOLUNTARY EUTHANASIA is when someone else, e.g. a doctor or a family member, decides that it would be in a person's best interest to end their life.

ACTIVE EUTHANASIA is when something is done to a person to make them die more quickly, e.g. giving drugs to bring about death.

PASSIVE EUTHANASIA is when any form of treatment that might extend a person's life is taken away, e.g. turning off a life-support machine or removing a feeding tube. N.B. In Britain today this is allowed. It would not legally be termed euthanasia.

I People who are worried about euthanasia talk of any concession being like a 'slippery slope'. What do you think this means?

ACTIVITY

Read the seven scenarios in Source A.

1 Read the Checkpoint on page 30. Which of the situations in Source A would not be regarded as euthanasia in Britain, so the person could legally be allowed to die?
2 Which situations would require active euthanasia and which passive euthanasia?
3 Organise the scenarios into two lists: those where *you* would approve of euthanasia and those where you would not.
4 Try to order your 'yes' list – the situations that most justify euthanasia will be at the top.
5 Now do the same with your 'no' list – this time the situation that *least* justifies euthanasia will be at the top.
6 Compare your lists with others. Defend your choices and your order.
7 As you thought about this, you will probably have said a number of times, 'It depends on whether...' Make a list of any extra considerations that you think are important in each case.
8 Carry out a class survey. What percentage agree with euthanasia in each situation? You can compare your class' opinions to the results in the actual British Social Attitudes Survey, which your teacher can give you.

SAVE AS...

9 Make your own list of arguments for and against euthanasia.

What does Judaism teach about euthanasia?

The sacred texts of Judaism all agree that euthanasia is wrong (see Sources B–D). In Judaism, euthanasia is seen as suicide if performed by individuals themselves, or murder if administered by another individual. Free will does not extend either to taking your own life or to asking someone else to end it.

Orthodox Jews would take the view that every effort should always be made to continue life.

Reform Jews would see a distinction between taking life and not prolonging life. If withdrawing medical help would lead to but not directly cause someone's death, this could be acceptable (see the interview with Rabbi Jonathan Wittenberg on pages 32–3).

B

One who is in a dying condition is regarded as a living being in all respects.

Mishnah

SAVE AS...

In order for euthanasia to be made legal in Britain, parliament would have to vote to change the law. Imagine you are a Jew whose MP is undecided on this issue. Write a letter urging your MP to oppose euthanasia and give reasons for your argument.

C

Despite yourself you were born, despite yourself you live, despite yourself you die, despite yourself you will hereafter have account and reckoning before the King of Kings, the Holy One, blessed be He.

Ethics of the Fathers 4.29. This is a section of Mishnah that is said daily as part of the morning service.

D

He who closes the eyes of a dying person while the soul is still departing is shedding blood. This may be compared to a lamp that is going out; if a man places his finger upon it, it is immediately extinguished.

Talmud

Compassion for the dying; care for the dying – a Jewish alternative to euthanasia

A hospice looks after people who are terminally ill. They are cared for by a wide range of trained medical staff. Their pain is relieved through drugs. Any fears about death that they or their families may have can be talked about with hospice staff or chaplains.

Rabbi Jonathan Wittenberg is the co-ordinator of the chaplaincy team at the North London Hospice. He is also community rabbi at the New North London Synagogue, a Masorti synagogue.

What is it like to work at a hospice?

This is not a Jewish hospice. The approach at this hospice is unique. The chaplains are from different religions, the patients too. So every chaplain usually sees every patient.

People often say to me that the hospice must be the worst part of my work, but that's far from the case. As chaplains, we are privileged because people here are searching for meanings, facing the big issues of life, and we are needed. I often feel that I am sharing something important. People are touched to the heart, and so little in life is on that level.

The chaplains are all part-time volunteers, so it's the nurses who are there in the middle of the night, when the real questions often get asked, when spiritual care is most needed. A big part of our chaplains' role is to help the staff develop their skills, so that they can help the very ill and their families to use the end of life to live, and to prepare for the 'transition', which is dying.

How can you help people prepare for death?

On a practical level, this can include setting the house in order. On a religious level, it is preparing to meet one's maker. I remember somebody who felt they had a lot of guilt on their conscience asking me what God's judgement would be, because Judaism teaches that there is judgement with mercy. There's a Jewish tradition of confessing before you die, although you don't want people to say: 'Now the rabbi's here, things are really bad!' I say to them, 'Many have confessed and gone on to live, and others have not confessed and died.'

What do you believe about life after death?

Traditional Judaism has two teachings on the question of what happens beyond the grave: the resurrection of the dead and the eternal life of the soul. I think that many Jews today are more comfortable with the eternity of the soul than with the resurrection of the body, although I know that other people feel differently from me.

I remember someone who was worried that they would be buried in a cemetery where they had no relatives, because they were afraid of the loneliness. But questions about the afterlife are asked more often after death by the family, who want to know where their loved one has gone, than by the dying person themselves.

But if someone asks me what will happen after death, I answer not as a theologian but as someone who cares for the person asking and tries to see their needs. I would generally say that it's a mystery. That Judaism does believe in the continuation of life after death, but it's not given to us to know much about it. It is a mystery that belongs with God. **Judaism is strongly rooted in this life.** It is a 'here and now' religion that focuses on practical ethical behaviour now, rather than on rewards in the life to come.

Do you get asked for advice by relatives?

After a death has taken place Jewish tradition provides a very clearly structured and, by wide consent, highly supportive process of bereavement (see page 26). The community gives the family a great deal of practical and spiritual support. The lead-up to a death doesn't have the same structure. And as doctors give families more say in the way a dying relative is treated, they need someone with whom they can share their dilemma. And I do find that Jewish people are choosing the rabbi.

For example, somebody was dying of heart failure. There were two daughters, one at the hospital, one at home. I happened to be at the hospital at that time. It was quite clear that the position of the hospital was, 'We have to ask you if you want your parent resuscitated, but we strongly recommend that you don't.' The sister who was there understood that and could see the state of her parent, but the sister at home said, 'Definitely resuscitate.' I could see that that was wrong. There was no doubt, it was as clear-cut as these things can be. In the event we spoke to the other sister again, who said, 'Do what you think has to be done.' A few minutes later the person died, and no one questioned the decision. That person could have been attached to some sort of machine to labour their breath for a few more hours. It was just not right. But it's very unusual for me to have such a pivotal role.

I Rabbi Jonathan Romain says, 'Judaism has never had a clear map of the afterlife.'
a) What do you think he means?
b) Would Rabbi Jonathan Wittenberg agree with him?

What is your view on euthanasia?

Interestingly, in all my time as a rabbi, even at the hospice, I have never been asked about euthanasia by a dying person or their family. It just isn't an issue.

There is a strong guiding principle in Jewish teaching that you don't take away hope. Some take this to mean that you never admit that a person is dying, and that you treat and treat and treat. Many ultra-Orthodox Jews hold this view, but this is not my understanding of Jewish sources. I've been researching what hope means to a person with a terminal illness. It can mean simply hoping to live long enough to see a certain event. I've found that many things coexist in the mind of someone who is dying. The notion that a person either knows that they're going to be cured or they know that they're going to die is just not right. They have days when they are very aware they are going to die and days when what's uppermost in their mind is hope and the future. Anyone caring for them has to respect that.

Sometimes people do wish to die. I was visiting a man once, not a hospice case, a very elderly man who was in a long period of decline. He was lonely, depressed and senile, the tragedy of our age in a way, and said, 'Pray for me to die' – a very difficult thing to do when you're with somebody.

There is a famous story in the Talmud. Rabbi Judah the Prince, a very great rabbi, was very ill. His maid, who knew him well, said, 'Up there in heaven the angels want him, and down here his pupils are praying for him. May it be God's will that the prayers of those below be stronger than the prayers of those on high.'

But then she saw his intense suffering and said, 'May it be God's will that the prayers of those on high be stronger than the prayers of those below.' And she dropped a jug, which shattered, distracting the people praying, and in the moment's quiet, he died. And the Talmud records no criticism of her for this. In fact, it comes to the conclusion, based on this and one other passage, that it is OK to pray for someone to die.

ACTIVITY

A hospice wishes to appoint a Jewish chaplain to work with sick and dying patients and their families.

1 Make a list of the skills and qualities that you feel are necessary for the job. You will need to read these two pages carefully.
2 Write a job advertisement, stressing the skills and qualities you require.
3 Write five questions that you will ask at the interview, which will help you to find the right person for the job.

FOCUS TASK

Write a brief guide for the chaplaincy team at a hospice on Jewish attitudes to euthanasia.

2.4 How do Jews make up their minds about capital punishment?

A

Amy Grossberg *was only eighteen in 1996 when she found herself pregnant. She was a student at the University of Delaware in the USA. She came from a stable and well-off Jewish family living in New Jersey.*

She did not tell her family that she was pregnant. Nor did she have an abortion. Her classmates noticed her pregnancy but said nothing because she did not mention it.

She asked no one for help. She panicked. When the baby was due she and her boyfriend **Brian Peterson** *delivered the baby themselves in a motel room, wrapped the baby in plastic and left it in a skip. They returned to their colleges.*

Later that evening Amy fainted in her college dormitory. An ambulance was called, and at hospital it was found that she had given birth only hours earlier. A search was on for the baby, and police sniffer dogs found the baby's body the next day.

Amy and Brian were both arrested. At first they said the baby had been born dead. Medical experts said the baby had died from a trauma to the head.

The couple were put on trial for murder. They pleaded innocent. Delaware allows capital punishment for murder. The Delaware Attorney General said that he would definitely press for the death penalty in this case.

✓ CHECKPOINT
Capital punishment in the UK

Until 1965 people in Britain could be hanged for murder.

In 1965 capital punishment was abolished for a trial period of five years. At the end of the trial period it was permanently abolished for murder. It was kept for treason, piracy on the high seas and burning Her Majesty's shipyards, so there is still a gallows at one English prison.

One of the last people to be executed in Britain was James Hanratty, who was hanged on 4 April 1962 for murdering a man and raping and shooting the man's lover in a layby on the A6 (the 'A6 murder'). In March 1999 his case was reopened by the Court of Appeal because of grave doubts about the conduct of the trial. He was pardoned.

Since 1965 many people have argued that capital punishment should be brought back for child-killers, serial killers and terrorists. Since 1970 Parliament has voted four times on whether to reintroduce the death penalty for murder. It has been rejected every time by a large majority.

In the 1960s there were 100–150 murders in Britain each year. In the 1990s there were around 700 murders each year.

B

During the Second World War **Adolf Eichmann** *was head of Jewish Affairs at Gestapo headquarters in Nazi Germany. He became the central figure in the 'Final Solution'. His job was to transport Jews from all over Europe to death camps where they were gassed or worked to death.*

At the end of the war many Nazi leaders committed suicide. Eichmann did not. He escaped from Europe and settled in Argentina.

In 1960 Israeli secret agents tracked him down and brought him to Israel. He stood trial for crimes against the Jewish people and crimes against humanity, was found guilty and executed.

DISCUSS
1 Read Source A. If Amy and Brian are found guilty of murder do you think that either of them should be executed? Give reasons. Your teacher can tell you what actually happened.
2 Read Source B. Do you think Adolf Eichmann should have been executed? Give reasons.
3 Does anyone in your class think that capital punishment is never right? Give reasons.

ACTIVITY A

The aims of punishment

Almost everyone agrees that people who have committed a crime should be punished in some way. But anyone deciding on a punishment has to consider what they are trying to achieve by it.

1 Here are some possible aims of punishment and a list of definitions. Match each one to the correct definition. It may help you to write each aim and each definition on separate slips of paper. Use a dictionary if you need to.

AIMS	DEFINITIONS
Deterrence	• for the safety of society, offenders may need to be put where they can't offend again
Retribution	• to help the offender become a better person
Reparation	• to discourage the offender (and other potential offenders) from committing similar crimes
Reform	• to offer revenge for those who have been wronged, society may want the offender to suffer
Protection	• to allow the offender to 'pay' for what they have done and have their guilt wiped away in order to make a fresh start
Vindication	• to uphold the authority and status of the law. Sometimes society wants to punish offenders to ensure that a law is taken seriously

SAVE AS . . .

2 Write out or paste the aims with the correct definitions in a table like this:

Aim	Definition	Capital punishment?

3 In the final column write a sentence to explain how far capital punishment can fulfil each aim.

ACTIVITY B

Working out your own views

Part of the aim of this course is for you to work out your own views and be able to explain them. So try out our 'capital punishment decision-maker':

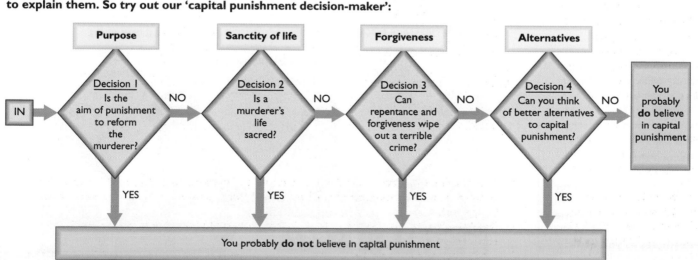

What does Judaism teach about capital punishment?

✓ CHECKPOINT
On page 19 you looked at the different attitudes of Orthodox and Reform Jews to the Torah. Capital punishment is a good example to illustrate how this affects their approach to real-life issues:

Orthodox Jews

defend the principle of capital punishment

because of their belief in the Torah as *authoritative*,

containing *absolute* truth.

They apply the Torah's support for capital punishment *literally*

and see it as a source of *changeless revelation*.

Reform Jews

vary in their views on capital punishment

because of their belief in the Torah as *guidance*,

containing *relative* truth.

They apply *reason and experience* to the Torah's teaching on capital punishment

and see it as a source of *continuing revelation*.

To complicate this simplified picture, however, although Orthodox Jews would defend the principle of capital punishment, in most cases the **absolute** principle of the sanctity of life would override any decision to execute.

SAVE AS...

Record the information in the Checkpoint as a table. It will be useful for revision.

   You can use the same 'format' to record further examples as you work through this course.

Principle 1: capital punishment is allowed

'You shall not murder' (Exodus 20.13) is the sixth of the Ten Commandments.

   By destroying the sacred life of another person a murderer has offended God and forfeited their right to live. Early Hebrew texts require the death penalty for murder. 'If anyone kills any human being, he shall be put to death.' (Leviticus 24.17)

   The early texts also consider punishable by death other offences that would not be considered serious today, such as adultery or insulting your father or mother (see Leviticus 20).

Principle 2: punishment should be proportional to the crime

The phrase 'eye for eye, tooth for tooth' (Exodus 21.24) has become a punishment 'catchphrase'. In popular opinion this is evidence to support retribution, particularly in the case of murder – a killer should be killed; a life for a life. However, this principle has *never* been taken literally in Jewish law. It has always been applied to guide levels of financial compensation, i.e. how much money the criminal should pay to the victim. In fact, the main aim of this principle is to prevent people *over*punishing or reacting to a small injury by inflicting a greater one on the offender. Jewish belief in the sanctity of life (see page 24) has always affected application of the death penalty, even in cases where execution would be legal under Jewish law. Which brings us to the third principle . . .

Principle 3: capital punishment should be a last resort

The main purpose of Jewish law is that God should be honoured and worshipped. Another practical purpose was to keep society stable and protect the individual from exploitation. This is the case for laws about punishment as for many others. Since God balances justice and mercy, punishment needs a balance of justice and mercy.

   The Mishnah records many restrictions on the use of capital punishment. For example, the death penalty could only be imposed after a trial by a Sanhedrin (Jewish Council) of 23 judges. According to the Talmud, circumstantial evidence is not acceptable (e.g. someone saying 'I saw the accused carrying a knife and walking towards . . .'). A confession by the accused cannot be accepted as evidence!

C

From a conversation recorded in Mishnah Makkot 1.10

Case study: the execution of Adolf Eichmann

In 1948 the new State of Israel decided not to allow capital punishment, even for murder. In 1962, however, it tried and convicted Adolf Eichmann for his role in the mass murder of the Shoah. (You considered his case on page 34.)

After Eichmann was found guilty, there were those in Israel who felt execution was the only possible punishment. There were others who felt that executing Eichmann would damage Israel. You can read the views of one leading Jewish scholar, Samuel Hugo Bergmann, in Source D.

D

Letter 1

I utterly oppose the death penalty in any form.

That people learned in law would sit together tranquilly and decide, with cold and objective consideration, that a man should be hanged – and that not they, but some other man paid a fee for it, would hang him – that is in my eyes the utmost cruelty. Who gave them permission to take life, and in so doing to take from the defendant the possibility of doing penance for his sins while he is still in this world? Only he who creates life has the authority to take life . . . The horrible deeds were performed by the defendant nearly twenty years ago, in entirely different historical and psychological circumstances . . . I do not know if he has indeed repented. I do not want to [limit] his crimes, but a great change has occurred in the world since then . . .

As for the man himself, the death penalty is a much more lenient punishment than lifetime imprisonment in an Israeli jail. Given the horrible crime he committed, there is no fit punishment for him; but in any case, the death penalty is the most lenient. The main point in my eyes: I am concerned for the soul of Israel . . .

I believe with perfect faith that the Holy One, Blessed Be He, has chosen us to be a light unto the gentiles [and] . . . that clemency for this man will halt the chain of hatred and bring the world a bit of salvation. Equally certain am I that a death sentence carried out will increase the hatred in the world – hatred against us and our hatred against other people – and will help the devil with a great victory in the world.

From a letter Bergmann wrote to three of his former students

Letter 2

We are not pleading for his life, because we know that no man is less worthy than he is of mercy, and we are not asking you to pardon him. We ask your decision [not to execute him] for the sake of our country and for the sake of our people. Our belief is that concluding Eichmann's trial with his execution will diminish the image of the Holocaust and falsify the historical and moral significance of this trial . . .

Carrying out a death sentence will make it possible for them to claim that the crime of the Nazis has been paid for, that blood ransom has been paid to the Jewish people for the blood that was shed. Let us not lend our hands to this; let us not agree, or even imply that we agree, that it is possible to ransom the sacrifice of six million by the hanging of this evil man.

After Eichmann had been sentenced to death, Bergmann and nineteen others sent this letter to the President of Israel. Most of those who signed it were university professors, born in Europe, who had survived the Shoah

Bergmann's second letter was unsuccessful. The Israeli press scorned his letter saying: 'A Pardon for Eichmann? No! Six Million Times No!' Eichmann was executed on 31 May 1962. Eichmann is the only person to be executed in Israel since its foundation in 1948.

FOCUS TASK

1 Read both letters in Source D carefully.
   a) List the different arguments that Bergmann uses against capital punishment.
   b) In one colour mark those arguments that are specific to Holocaust criminals, in another colour those that could apply to the punishment of any murderer.
2 Do you agree or disagree with Bergmann's view? Explain why.
3 Bergmann is no longer alive, but imagine you can write him a letter explaining *your* views on capital punishment. Show that you have considered other points of view.

Issues of life and death – Review tasks

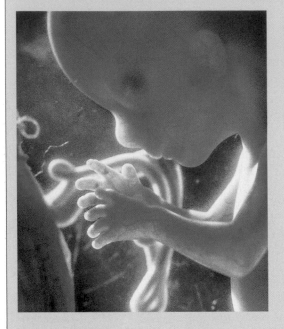

1   What name would be given to the deliberate taking of life in each of the pictures on this page?

2   For each one, explain whether Judaism would:

   • always forbid it
   • in some cases forbid it, in others allow it
   • always allow individuals to decide.

3   Summarise what Jews believe about the sanctity of life. Support your answer with examples from Jewish texts and rituals.

Judy Buenuano, the 'Black Widow', spent thirteen years on Death Row in Florida before being executed in 1998 for the murder of her husband in 1971.

UNIT 3

Relationships

If I am not for myself, who will be for me ?

And if I am only for myself, what am I ?

And if not now, when ?

Hillel said this in the first century CE.

Your relationships connect you to other people. Have you ever thought about the number of people with whom you have a relationship? There are probably hundreds, from your close family, through friends, to acquaintances you see only rarely.

What effect do you have on the lives of other people now? What effect will you have in the future?

What kind of a child, sibling, friend, student, acquaintance are you? What kind of a partner, friend, parent could you be? What effect will you have on the lives of your neighbours? What kind of employer or employee will you be?

In this unit you will explore some of these issues. You will be asked to think about your answers to these questions and respond to the ways different Jews might answer them.

3.1   Why do Jews say people should marry?

ACTIVITY

1   Complete this sentence in your own way: 'The ideal family is . . .'
2   Compare your ideas with those of other members of your class. What do you agree and disagree about?

DISCUSS A

1   After you have studied these two pages, discuss as a class whether the ideal Jewish family is similar to or different from your ideal.
2   What do you think are the advantages and disadvantages of the strong emphasis on family life within Judaism?

Why is the family so important in Judaism?

Family life is like a glue that holds Judaism together.

All Jews are expected to marry, to have at least two children (a boy and a girl) and to bring these children up to follow Jewish traditions and customs. Mothers and fathers, especially mothers, have a key role in transmitting Jewish values to their children. They are expected to create a secure and nurturing environment for the children; a worshipping environment where children learn to pray and to worship God; a teaching environment where children develop as individuals and learn the ways of Judaism.

DO AS I DO

The fifth Commandment instructs Jews to respect their father and mother. Children in a Jewish family are strongly expected to contribute to family life and fulfil their parents' hopes for them. Loyalty to family is highly prized.

TOGETHERNESS

Many of the Jewish festivals revolve around eating meals together as a family. Every Friday night Shabbat is welcomed with family prayers, a family meal, fun and sharing (see page 4). Celebrating these festivals is an essential part of family life. Even children who have grown up and have left home often return home for Friday night. Many non-observant Jews (those who have stopped going to synagogue and who do not hold the traditional beliefs of Judaism) celebrate these festivals with their family as the only link with their Jewish roots.

In Reform synagogues men and women do not sit separately (see page 54). Many Reform Jews appreciate being able to sit with their family to pray and sing.

SIZE MATTERS

The first commandment in the Torah (Genesis 1.28) is 'Go forth and multiply', so Jewish couples are traditionally encouraged to have as many children as possible. Among ultra-Orthodox Jews, ten or more children is not unusual.

CARE

In the UK most Jews live as nuclear families, some as extended families, but almost all would feel a duty to care for their elderly or sick relatives. At Purim special food parcels are prepared to give to family, friends and Jewish people in need of food, treats or company.

WELCOMING STRANGERS

Inevitably, not all Jews have families of their own. There is a strong feeling among Jews that they should invite into their families other Jews who are alone, especially on Friday nights and for the Jewish festivals. At Passover (see page 102) Jews are reminded to consider the needs of others, and that company is as much of a need as food.

> **Whoever is hungry – let them come and eat! Whoever is needy – let them come and celebrate Passover!**

RITES OF PASSAGE

There are rituals to mark each stage in family life. When a son is eight days old there is the ritual of BRIT MILAH (circumcision). When a person is married the whole family celebrates together (see page 44). When someone dies the whole family joins in a shared mourning process (see page 26). These customs strengthen the bonds between family members. Events that affect one individual are seen as events for the whole family.

SAVE AS...

Record in your own words, with examples, how a Jewish family helps preserve Jewish traditions and values. You could use these headings:

- large families
- strong relationships
- home-based rituals.

DISCUSS B

Jews are famous for their jokes. Telling jokes and funny stories about themselves is an old Jewish tradition. The mother's role in family life is so strong that she crops up in many 'Jewish mother' jokes. Here are two examples:

> What is the difference between a Rottweiller and a Jewish mother?

> The Rottweiller eventually lets go.

and

> What is the difference between a Jewish mother and a terrorist?

> With a terrorist you can negotiate terms.

1 Do you think these jokes are funny?
2 Do you think they are cruel?
3 What point are these jokes making?

How to choose a partner

Jews are expected to marry and have children. However, they are encouraged to marry even if they will not be able to have children, since humans need companionship. God made Eve as a companion for Adam. Marriage is the ideal for all Jews. Judaism attaches no special status to celibacy.

It is no surprise that finding the right partner is taken very seriously by Jews. Indeed, at the spiritual level it is said that in marriage, 'God and his angels bring together two souls who were intended for each other even before birth.'

The shadchan

Traditionally, Jewish families would arrange for their child to meet suitable prospective partners. To help with this task, it was common to use a SHADCHAN (matchmaker), and this is not unusual amongst the ultra-Orthodox even today. The couple are given the opportunity to get to know each other, and either party can refuse the match, but the marriage can be said to be 'arranged', in that the couple know that the prospective partner is looking for a lifetime commitment and will not be 'unsuitable' in a religious sense. In fact, in modern society some Jewish singles engage a shadchan to find themselves a partner (see www.schachtel.com/ for a description of a shadchan's work), and there are many Jewish dating organisations, including lots on the Internet, that aim to help Jews to meet other Jews.

A

Once a Roman matron asked Rabbi Jose:
'How long did it take the Holy One to create the world?'
He said, 'Six days.'
'And since then what has He been doing?'
'He is occupied in making marriages.'
'And that is His occupation?' the woman scoffed. 'Even I can do that.'
'It may appear easy in your eyes,' he said, 'yet every marriage is as difficult as dividing the Red Sea.'
Then Rabbi Jose left her and went on his way.
What did the matron do? She took a thousand men slaves and a thousand women slaves, placed them in two rows and said, 'This one should wed that one, and this one should wed that one.' In one night she married them all.
The next day they came before her – one with a wounded head, one with a bruised eye, another with a fractured arm and one with a broken foot.
'What is the matter with you?' she asked.
Each one said, 'I do not want the one you gave me.'
Immediately the woman sent for Rabbi Jose and said to him,
'Rabbi, your Torah is true, beautiful and praiseworthy.'
'Indeed a suitable match may seem easy to make, yet God considers it as difficult a task as dividing the Red Sea,' Rabbi Jose acknowledged.

MIDRASH, Genesis Rabbah 68.4

B

When you choose a wife, remember that she is to be your companion in life, in building up your home, in the performance of your life task, and choose accordingly. It should not be wealth or physical beauty or brilliance of mind that makes you decide whom to marry. Rather, look for richness of heart, beauty of character, and good sense and intelligence. If, in the end, you require money, and your wife's family freely offers it to you, you may take it; but woe to you and your future household if you are guided only by considerations of money.

Rabbi Samson Raphael Hirsch (1808–88)

The Lord God said, 'It is not good for man to be alone; I will make a fitting helper for him.'

Genesis 2.18

1 What mistakes did the Roman matron in Source A make?
2 Do you think Source B is good advice? Give reasons.
3 Reread Source B, substituting 'husband/he' for 'wife/she'. Is it good advice? Give reasons.
4 Should you take other people's help or advice over whom to marry? List the advantages and disadvantages of doing so.

SAVE AS...

1 Draw up your own 'checklist' of questions to ask yourself about a possible marriage partner.
2 Mark the questions that might also appear on a Jewish checklist. Your teacher can then show you a list compiled by an Orthodox rabbi, to see whether you agree with him.

Why are Jews concerned about 'marrying out'?

Traditionally, the most important quality in a marriage partner was that he/she had to be Jewish. But in the UK today, 44 per cent of Jewish men 'marry out', that is, they marry non-Jewish women. The rate for Jewish women is only slightly lower.

The statistics show that intermarried couples are less likely to keep Jewish practices, more likely to divorce, and there is less chance that their children will feel Jewish or marry a Jew. Such couples have been accused by some of giving Hitler a posthumous victory, or at least of breaking a 4000-year-long chain of continuity. The fear is that if Jews continue to marry non-Jews the community will decline and eventually vanish.

C

Is intermarriage a new phenomenon?

Jewish outmarriage has always existed, although there was a real leap in the 1930s when war and evacuation took lots of young Jewish East Londoners to non-Jewish areas.

What problems does it cause?

The couple's families may react with hostility and disappointment when faced with the prospect of having intermarried children. Instead of congratulations, the couple receive scowls. Once married, they have to decide how to deal with many day-to-day issues: religious festivals, life-cycle events, even their own funerals. The children's upbringing is an extra dimension. Many people underestimate their religious feelings. When they become parents, they want to recreate the sights and smells of their own childhood. Do you circumcise your son or baptise him? Is a Christmas tree just decoration, or a declaration of domestic war? Marrying a Jew versus 'marrying out' was once described to me as the difference between slipping into a warm or a cold bath.

Are such children brought up as Jews?

In the past, the Jewish community reacted to outmarrying Jews with hostility, assuming that they were deliberately opting out. These people felt ostracised, and therefore didn't bring up their children as Jews. If the mother was Christian, they didn't feel the child was even eligible. We now know these Jews fell in love with a non-Jew accidentally, as an inevitable part of living in an assimilated society, so the community has become more welcoming. At the moment, though, a high proportion of these children are brought up with little or no Jewish knowledge or identity.

So what's the solution?

There is no solution, because Jews will continue meeting and falling in love with non-Jews. Rather than deny the issue or condemn it, the Jewish community must take a more positive attitude, and make the best of an undesirable situation. Lots of Jews who marry out want to feel part of the Jewish community and pass on the heritage. A lot depends on whether the community helps or hinders them. Conversion is an option for those who want it, and we need to make the process less of an obstacle course. But mainly we should be accepting the partner as they are, and making them feel welcome in the synagogue. Forty years of rabbinical condemnation hasn't worked, because the rate of intermarriage is increasing. It is even counter-productive, because it ensures that the Jewish partner doesn't want to have any more to do with Jewish life.

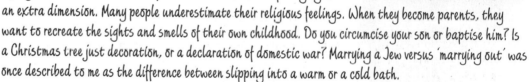

Jonathan Romain is rabbi of Maidenhead Synagogue, a Reform synagogue. He works with many intermarried couples and their families.

A Jewish wedding

Different Jewish traditions celebrate weddings in different ways, but there are certain common factors.

What is needed for a Jewish wedding?

1　An object of established value for the groom to give his bride. Usually this is a **ring**, which must be a plain band of metal with no holes, engraving or gemstones and must belong to the groom.
2　A marriage **contract** (a KETUBAH). The text dates back to the second century BCE and is written in Aramaic (an ancient Middle-Eastern language). It spells out the rights of the married woman to be supported and cherished by her husband.
3　Two eligible **witnesses** to observe the ceremony, which takes place under the CHUPAH (wedding canopy).

Source D lists the conventional ingredients. The chupah, the witnesses and steps 5, 6 and 7 are *legal* requirements of Jewish law. You would find these in all Jewish weddings. The rest have grown out of tradition.

D

Running order

1　Veiling (BEDEKEN)

2　The procession

3　Circling the groom

4　Blessings

5　Giving of ring by groom

6　Reading of the ketubah

7　Seven blessings

8　Breaking a glass

9　The couple retire

The couple are escorted to the chupah by their parents.

The bride walks seven times round the groom.

Over a cup of wine and for the betrothal.

He puts the ring on the bride's right index finger, and, observed by two witnesses, says, 'Behold you are consecrated to me with this ring according to the Law of Moses and Israel.'

This marriage contract is then presented to the bride.

Given to the couple, often by their family and friends.

The groom's stamping on a glass symbolises that no joy can be complete since the destruction of the Temple in Jerusalem.

They go to a room for their first moment of privacy as a married couple.

E

The groom lowers the bride's veil himself, having made sure she is the right woman!

F

The marriage takes place under the chupah, a cloth supported by four poles. This represents the couple's future home which, like Abraham's tent, should be open to visitors.

G

The bride and groom wear white as a symbol of purity and of new life.

44

H

Traditionally, the ceremony is followed by a celebration and festive meal at which friends and family rejoice and dance with the bride and groom. These Jews are from the Yemen.

I

At an Orthodox wedding men and women dance separately. Sometimes the wedding is followed by seven days of celebration by the couple and community.

J

A ketubah by calligrapher and artist Vetta Alexis. Ketubot provide almost limitless opportunities for imaginative decoration, both traditional and modern.

1   Why is the presence of witnesses so important?
2   Look up Genesis 29.16–27. What is the connection between this story and the custom of bedeken?
3   It is a mitzvah (commandment) to make a Jewish wedding and celebration as joyful and beautiful as possible. Suggest ways this could be done.
4   Choose three aspects of the wedding and explain how they can help bond a couple together at the start of their married life.

✓ CHECKPOINT

Sex

Jewish teachings on sex focus almost entirely on the relationship between husband and wife. Sex outside marriage is not permitted.

A married relationship is an emotional, intellectual, spiritual and physical union.

'When a man and his wife unite sexually in holiness, the SHECHINAH [the Presence of God] rests between them.'

(Maimonides, referring to Talmud, Sotah 17a)

Judaism sees sex, within the holiness of a marriage, as something joyful in its own right. It is to be enjoyed, and by both participants; the man is specifically required to satisfy his wife. She has this right even if she is pregnant, past the menopause or infertile for any reason. The Talmud, written in the early centuries of the first millennium, even goes so far as to detail how often a husband must give his wife sex.

Family purity and mikvah

A traditional Jewish marriage is governed by rituals regarding 'family purity'. This means that sex between a husband and wife is not permitted whilst the woman is menstruating or for seven days afterwards. To mark the end of this period each month, and to symbolically prepare her for reunion with her husband she visits the MIKVAH (ritual bath). This is a small, four-foot deep pool of 'living' water that must come – at least partially – from rain. Having first washed, the woman immerses herself completely in the mikvah three times, reciting a blessing after the first.

The mikvah is also used at other times in Jewish life: by a new convert, by a bride before her wedding, by a mother after giving birth, and sometimes by men on the eve of the Sabbath and festivals.

Kosher sex

Shmuley Boteach is an Orthodox rabbi. He was Director of the educational organisation L'Chaim Society (means 'life'). He has earned an international reputation as a speaker, broadcaster and writer.

His book *Kosher Sex* (see Source K for extracts and Source L for cover) was a surprise bestseller. Kosher means 'acceptable to God.' In *Kosher Sex* he guides Jewish and non-Jewish readers into the Jewish understanding of sex. He celebrates sex as a powerful bond between husband and wife. He also celebrates the wisdom of the Torah in establishing clear principles and patterns for a sexual relationship, which are as relevant today as they ever were.

K

1 What is sex for?

There are three possibilities as to what sex is for: pleasure, procreation, or oneness. Judaism, believing that the path to holiness is always to be found in the 'golden middle', rejects the far right extreme of 'sex-is-only-for-babies'. Neither does Judaism embrace the extreme secular view that sex is for fun and pleasure. Rather, Judaism says that the purpose of sex is to knit two strangers together as one. Sex is the ultimate bonding process.

What few of us seem to realise today is that the yearning for emotional intimacy is as real as the hunger for food and water, shelter and clothing. Animals may copulate and then separate, but humans are radically different. We have sex with our minds awake. What goes on in our bodies is not enough.

2 Why am I writing about sex?

Being a rabbi to young people, the principal subject that arises is relationships. But the real reason I write about sex is an idealistic one. I write about sex because it is holy. It is as religious a subject as a discussion on belief in God. It is only through sex that a soul is brought into this world, that a man and woman merge as one, as they were before creation, and it is one of the few mystical experiences that we all share. Young people today are deprived because to them sex is only physical.

3 How to combine intimacy and passion: fire and water

In my years of counselling couples I have encountered two types of marriage. There are couples who share every secret and depend on each other utterly. They are inseparable. They have intimacy. So what's their problem? There is little or no passion. Theirs is a love like water, not like fire. Since there is no flame, their marriage is predictable.

Then there are the husbands and wives who are lovers. Theirs is a passionate fiery union. They fight and argue constantly. They do not, however, completely love or even trust each other. There is nothing dull about their marriage, but it is like a guitar whose strings are strung too tightly.

The problem is that for a marriage to be successful it must somehow fuse these opposites – a marriage needs fire and water. But how can we achieve both simultaneously? This is what kosher sex is all about.

Recognising this dilemma, the Bible, more than three millennia ago, ingeniously offered the following solution. Every month there must be two weeks devoted to physical love, and two weeks devoted to intellectual communication and emotional intimacy. And what better cycle to follow than the exact rhythm of the female body? For two weeks the couple unite physically and forge deep bonds. When the woman's period begins, the two weeks are up – just before monotony sets in. For twelve days the couple must abstain from sex (see Checkpoint). They must focus on discovering the personality, not the flesh.

As the days pass by they hunger for one another. Their desire replenishes itself until, twelve days after they have separated, their love for one another reaches its crescendo and their inner fire and passion leap out like the eruption of a volcano.

They enjoy a monthly honeymoon when they discover each other's bodies as if for the first time.

4 Kosher sex in a nutshell

- Great sex has you focused on the body of your partner, but **kosher sex** has you bound with the soul of your lover.
- Great sex promotes physical exhilaration, but **kosher sex** leads to spiritual integration.
- Great sex is an end to an encounter, but **kosher sex** is the beginning of a relationship.

L

Kosher Sex by Shmuley Boteach

DISCUSS

Look carefully at Source L.
1 What impression does it give you of sex?
2 What point do you think the artist is making?
3 Why do you think it was chosen for the cover of *Kosher Sex*?

Read the extracts in Source K.
4 What do these extracts tell you about the place of sex within a relationship?
5 Do you think this advice is valuable only for Jews, or for non-Jews as well?

SAVE AS...

6 Write a paragraph explaining what you find most helpful and least helpful in Jewish guidance on sex.

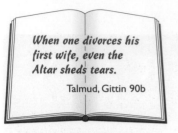

When one divorces his first wife, even the Altar sheds tears.

Talmud, Gittin 90b

Divorce procedure

1 The court questions both spouses to check, repeatedly, that they both consent to the divorce. The questions and responses, to the scribe and witnesses as well as to the couple, must be followed like a script.

2 The husband authorises the scribe to write him a GET ('document').

3 The witnesses sign it.

4 The husband receives the get from the rabbi, and gives it to the wife with both hands, saying in Hebrew and English, 'This be your get and with it be you divorced from this time forth so that you may become the wife of any man.'

5 The wife receives it with open palms. She lifts her hands to show possession, walks with it a short distance, turns, and gives it back to the rabbi.

6 The four corners of the get are cut to indicate it has been used and cannot be re-used. It is kept by the court, the couple being issued instead with a release form. This indicates that they are now divorced and free to remarry. The woman, though, must wait 92 days, to prevent doubts over the paternity of any newly-conceived child.

Is contraception allowed?

Three principles affect Jewish attitudes to contraception:

1 Jews are required to 'be fruitful and multiply' (Genesis 1.28). This is the responsibility of the man, who is expected to father at least a boy and a girl – the minimum to replace the parents.
2 Sex is for pleasure as well as procreation.
3 Wasting seed (semen) is not permitted. Therefore, anything that impedes normal intercourse is forbidden.

The Orthodox and Reform traditions differ in their teaching on contraception.

The Orthodox tradition:
- emphasises how precious children are
- permits contraception only where pregnancy would pose a threat to the mother's life or health
- does not allow contraception for social or economic reasons (e.g. because a couple cannot afford another child)
- does not allow couples to use contraceptive methods that impede normal intercourse, such as the rhythm method (which involves abstaining from sex) or the condom (which wastes seed).

The Reform tradition:
- also emphasises the preciousness of children, particularly in the light of the many Jewish lives lost in the Shoah
- allows contraception for social or economic reasons
- allows individual Jews to choose which method to use.

Is divorce allowed?

Divorce is allowed in Judaism, even on the grounds of simple incompatibility. It is, though, viewed as the last resort. Only when reconciliation has been attempted and failed should this final step to separation be taken.

Terminating a relationship is viewed as sad, but not humiliating. Indeed, allowing for the possibility of divorce is an indication of the value Judaism places on marriage. If a couple can no longer love each other as 'one flesh', it is seen as better that they should part. Since there is no need to find one partner 'guilty', Jewish divorce is not a battle.

Only the husband can initiate and give a divorce, but the process requires his wife's consent. Just as the marriage was consecrated 'according to the Law of Moses and Israel', so it must be dissolved according to this law. A civil court does not have the power to divorce a couple in Jewish law (or vice versa).

The process of Jewish divorce originates in the Bible: 'A man takes a wife and possesses her. She fails to please him because he finds something obnoxious about her, and he writes her a bill of divorcement, hands it to her, and sends her away from his house.' (Deuteronomy 24.1)

Religious divorce takes place under the guidance of a Beth Din, a rabbinic Court of Law that is not part of the civil law courts. In the UK a couple also needs a civil divorce under British law (see Checkpoint on page 49).

The flowchart on the left makes divorce sound rather straightforward. In reality, of course, the breakdown of marriage is often an emotionally traumatic experience for the couple and any children.

✓ CHECKPOINT
Divorce law in Britain
In the nineteenth century you needed an Act of Parliament to be divorced. Since then it has become progressively easier and cheaper to obtain a civil divorce. The Divorce Reform Act (1971) removed the need for one of the couple to be the 'guilty party'. Since then, most divorces have been on the grounds of 'the irretrievable breakdown of the marriage'.

In 1984, the minimum period of marriage before a couple can seek a divorce was reduced from three years to one.

Every change in divorce legislation has resulted in an increase in the number of couples divorcing. More than 35 per cent of all marriages in Britain end in divorce, with Denmark being the only country in Europe with a higher rate.

I The divorce process mixes symbolism with legal processes. For each element 1–6 in the flowchart on page 48 explain what you think its purpose is.

M

Being a product of a broken home, it still bothers me that there are children of similar homes who will actually speak about their parent's divorce as if it were a good thing. Surely they are mistaken. Our parents would have been better off happily married.

My whole life has been affected by my parents' divorce. It heightened my insecurities and left me feeling that nothing in life really works. To me the world was made of a bunch of broken pieces. How else is a child to feel when the archetypal relationship, which brought him or her into this world, dissolves? Where would I eventually fit in? I looked forward neither to happiness, nor to peace. When a doctor recently asked me in synagogue if I thought that his recent divorce would have any effect on their son, I said, 'It's like asking whether discovering that the sun won't shine tomorrow, or that the body has no immune system, will have any affect on one's outlook on life.'

Shmuley Boteach in *Kosher Sex* (see page 46)

The 'chained woman'

A woman cannot initiate a Jewish divorce, so if a marriage has broken down she is dependent on her husband to give her a get (the divorce document). Without this she cannot marry another Jew, since in Jewish law she is still married. Any relationship she has will be regarded in Jewish law as adulterous and any children born from it illegitimate.

This situation has created AGUNOT (so-called 'chained women', singular is AGUNAH), who want a divorce, but whose husbands will not grant one.

Traditionally this situation would have been resolved within the Jewish community. Rabbis would try to persuade the husband that if the marriage was beyond repair, it was in the interests of his wife and children to grant a get. If he resisted, social pressure would have forced him to 'free' his wife.

In the modern world, where a husband might have moved to the other side of the world, it is more difficult. The Orthodox tradition is aware of the problem, but has not found a solution that is acceptable within Jewish law.

The Reform tradition has adapted the traditional legal process so that if the husband cannot be persuaded to grant his wife a get, the Beth Din gives her a document that allows her to remarry, so avoiding the agunah problem.

FOCUS TASK

Guidelines issued by the Marriage Authorisation Office of the Chief Rabbi suggest a rabbi meets the couple before the wedding ceremony to discuss their wedding and marriage.

Plan a leaflet that might be given to a Jewish couple at this interview, explaining:

* the purpose of a Jewish marriage
* how a wedding ceremony is conducted
* the mutual obligations of a husband and wife
* what happens should the marriage fail.

For the second point, remember that this advice to couples is from the Chief Rabbi. The wedding ceremony is essentially a religious service and a rabbi, while wishing where possible to accommodate the couple's preferences, must also see to it that Jewish law and custom are respected.

N

Orthodox Jewish women protesting against the situation of agunot outside the office of the Chief Rabbi in London

3.2 Is a Jewish woman's role less important than a man's?

DISCUSS

1 **As a class, brainstorm the following.**
   a) In one column, list evidence that men and women in the UK today are treated totally equally.
   b) In another column, list evidence that men and women in the UK today are not treated as equals.
2 **Which list is longest? Can you agree as a class – equal or not equal?**
3 **What is the difference between being 'equal' and being 'the same'?**

   Now let's see what you think about women in Judaism.
      Are they equal to men?
      Are they treated differently from men?

The Bible and the Talmud gave women more rights and protection than in other societies of the times. For example, a woman had to give her consent to a marriage and she was allowed to keep property she had owned as a single woman. The marriage contract ensured she had financial support from her husband.

However, these texts gave women different roles from men. The traditional view is that women's role is not inferior, just different. Women were given a special and sacred role as the childbearer, homemaker and transmitter of Jewish values. A Jewish woman's children are always considered Jewish, and she has the main responsibility for the children's Jewish upbringing. She transmits moral and ethical values, and encourages observance of Jewish practices.

Jewish law excuses women (over the age of twelve) from some religious duties, particularly those that need to be done at a certain time. However, they are given some specific duties that don't apply to men. For example,

Women are not obliged to:
- Wear TZIZIT and tephilin
- Pray three times a day
- Read the Torah at services

Women are specifically obliged to:
- Light the Shabbat candles
- Remove a small piece of dough when baking bread and burn it in memory of the Temple
- Keep menstrual purity

A

What a rare find is a capable wife!
Her worth is far beyond that of rubies.
Her husband puts his confidence in her,
And lacks no good thing.
She is good to him, never bad,
All the days of her life...
She is clothed with strength and splendour;
She looks to the future cheerfully.
Her mouth is full of wisdom,
Her tongue with kindly teaching.
She oversees the activities of her household
And never eats the bread of idleness.
Her children declare her happy;
Her husband praises her,
'Many women have done well,
But you surpass them all.'

From 'Eshet Chayil' (Proverbs 31.10–12, 25–9). At the Friday night meal the husband recites these verses to his wife. Eshet Chayil means 'a woman of worth'.

B

A girl at a Reform Synagogue receiving a blessing from the rabbi at her Bat Mitzvah.

Entering into the covenant: welcoming baby girls

In Judaism there are few public celebrations for women's life events. Traditionally, too, boys' life cycle events like brit milah (circumcision) and BAR MITZVAH (age thirteen) have had no equivalent for girls. For a number of years, though, many synagogues have been offering a BAT MITZVAH, for girls of twelve or thirteen, and a 'Baby Blessing' in the synagogue for newborn girls. Some families have created their own welcoming ceremonies for a daughter. In Hebrew the ceremony may be called a Simchat Bat (Joy of the Daughter) or Brit Bat (Covenant of the Daughter). There are no rules on how it should be done, so there is much scope for creativity.

C

MAZALTOV!

As new parents, or grandparents, of a beautiful baby girl, you would like to joyously and ceremoniously welcome her into your family, into the family of humanity, and into the Jewish family. Just as her brothers enter into the Jewish community through a Brit Milah, new daughters need to be brought into this enormous and enveloping Jewish family. Daughters also need to become partners in the Covenant between God and his people.

In recent times, many branches of Judaism have begun to fashion ceremonies which mark with equal zeal the birth of a girl, which celebrate the beginning of a new life, and bestow upon the child her Jewish name . . . All those gathered need to understand that, as witnesses, they are part of a ritual. That is why a script (in the form of a booklet) should be carefully prepared and distributed at a Simchat Bat ceremony.

Use the following outline of the various elements you might include in a ceremony as a guide.

- Welcoming the guests
- Welcoming the baby
- Prayers of thanksgiving
- Readings about God's love and trust of children
- Naming the baby
- Entering the baby into the Covenant
- Studying a passage of Torah
- Parental blessing
- Festive meal

By Rabbi Nina Beth Cardin

ACTIVITY

Write a welcoming ceremony for a Jewish baby girl, using the outline in Source C as a guide. You can include any texts you feel are appropriate.

DISCUSS

1 **On getting up each morning a traditionally observant Jewish man will, among other blessings, thank God 'for not having made me a woman'.**
   a) Why do you think he says this prayer?
   b) Why might some people object to it?

SAVE AS . . .

2 **Can you make up a blessing that people could say instead of this one? (Your teacher can tell you what some Jews do.)**

FOCUS TASK

Work in groups of four.
   In blessing their daughters, parents hope that they will become like Sarah, Rebecca, Rachel and Leah.
1 **Each look up one of their stories in the Bible: Genesis 18.1–15; 24.1–20; 27.1–23; 29.15–30.2.**
2 **List the qualities the woman displays.**
3 **Share your findings with your group. What qualities of each woman might parents want their daughters to acquire? Would they want the same qualities for their sons?**
4 **Use your lists to compile a group display entitled 'the ideal woman'.**

Women in the synagogue

Traditional Judaism has emphasised a woman's domestic role and downplayed her role in the synagogue rituals. For example, seeing women as by nature more 'spiritual' than men, it does not expect them to pray three times a day as men do. Women can, though, choose to do so. It is possible to argue that exempting women from some religious duties protected women who would have found it difficult to add these daily burdens to their domestic responsibilities.

There are other ritual practices from which women are in theory exempt. However, in practice exemption has come to mean forbidden to women, at least in Orthodox services. Orthodox synagogues do not accept a woman wearing a tallit or tephilin. She cannot lead a service or be called up to read from the Torah scroll. Because of this she cannot mark her Bat Mitzvah (Daughter of the Commandment) in the same way as a boy marks his Bar Mitzvah (Son of the Commandment) by being called up to read for the first time at thirteen.

The reason for all of these is based on the legal technicality that if a woman was to fulfil a ritual function that is required of a man, such as reading from the Torah, the implication would be that no man present was capable of doing it.

Some women accept these limitations on their role; others do not. In Reform Judaism women in the synagogue have equality with men, including the opportunity to become rabbis.

In Orthodox circles nowadays, many Jewish women are as well educated as men. Many choose to combine careers and religious obligations with the traditional large families.

Some also want to participate more fully in the ritual aspects of Jewish life than is permitted within a traditional Orthodox setting. They are not Reform, but they are used to participating as equals in all other aspects of their lives and are no longer happy to leave all this at the door when they enter an Orthodox synagogue.

SAVE AS...

Think about one Jewish duty that a man is required to do but a woman is not. In two columns list:
a) reasons why women might be exempt from this duty
b) reasons why you think some women want to do it.

D

The Jewish Women's Network
Action, Dialogue and Learning for Jewish Women Across the Spectrum

We aim to:

- Create a framework within which all Jewish women can engage in dialogue.

- Support endeavours among women across the spectrum to improve their status and participation in Jewish life.

- Develop and promote learning opportunities for Jewish women across the spectrum.

Founded in 1993, the Jewish Women's Network (JWN) is an independent forum for all Jewish women. We believe that such a forum provides a much needed voice for Jewish women's experiences and concerns.

The JWN is a support system of and for individual Jewish women. It is both a resource for Jewish women and a catalyst for change.

JWN recognises the importance of defining ourselves as individuals worthy of respect whatever our age, status or beliefs.

From a leaflet produced by the Jewish Women's Network

I Against the Chief Rabbi's instructions, the women's tefilah group (Source E) held a prayer service using a scroll. Do you think they were right to do this? Explain why or why not.

In the early 1990s, some members of the Jewish Women's Network were involved in setting up an Orthodox all-women TEFILAH (prayer) group. The group met much opposition within the United (Orthodox) Synagogue. Chief Rabbi Dr Jonathan Sacks ruled that they could meet to pray outside of synagogue premises, but that they were not allowed to use a SEFER TORAH (scroll) in their services. Despite this, they did hold a prayer service using a scroll, from which they read and chanted aloud.

E

WORSHIPPERS SHRUG OFF CONTROVERSY OVER DECISION TO IGNORE CHIEF RABBI'S BAN

'We are really making history,' says proud teenager at milestone Sefer Torah service

It looked like any women's gathering in any United synagogue. But Sunday's event marked an historic moment in Anglo-Jewry – the first-ever Orthodox women-only service to use a Sefer Torah.

Rays of sunlight filtered into the unexceptional-looking hall, as about 100 women, some of them accompanied by their children, congregated in a peaceful and dignified atmosphere.

It was a stark contrast to the heated controversy which had raged ever since the service was first mooted.

Outside the building, a police car was parked, summoned by the organisers who had feared a demonstration.

The irony was that the women, many of them long-time United Synagogue members, hardly looked like the kind of people who would provoke trouble.

They were modestly dressed – even more so than women in many Orthodox congregations – with blouses covering their shoulders and skirts below their knees. Sitting at the back were a number of women wearing snoods, a head garment associated with strict Orthodoxy.

But, despite their sober appearance, these were the women who had rocked the establishment by defying the Chief Rabbi in their determination to worship with a Sefer Torah.

The much-awaited moment finally arrived. With little ceremony, two women made their way towards the Ark and opened it.

The Sefer Torah was handed over to Mrs Kruger . . .

The last woman to read from the scroll was teenager Vicki Kruger. After the service, she described the excitement of the moment. "I felt really proud. It is something that will always have a place in my heart. We really are making history."

Afterwards, the women emerged clearly feeling a sense of pride and satisfaction. "It was a real spiritual fix – you don't get that elsewhere. I feel left out from most Orthodox services," one said.

"Women must take the opportunity to find out for themselves," said Ann Barnett.

"There was nothing to scandalise the most traditional women," another participant said.

A final word came from a member of Lauderdale Road Sephardi synagogue.

"It made you feel you were part of God's people," she said.

Valerie Monchi in the *Jewish Chronicle*, 18 March 1994

Some experiences of Jewish women

From Orthodox to Reform – and back again?

F

Lydia Burman

As a little girl I used to go to SHUL with my father. Although it was a very male environment and I felt different from that, I felt a part of it. Yet as I grew up and was relegated up to the women's gallery I felt increasingly estranged. At home, Jewish knowledge was not deliberately withheld, but as a girl others decided for me that some things were not important for me to know.

There is a sense of a rhythm to Jewish life. At my secondary school 60 per cent of the kids were Jewish. They knew the rules but had no feeling for Judaism or knowledge of why they were keeping it – the opposite of me, who knew why but chose not to keep.

As a single Jewish woman I felt there was no place for me in an Orthodox synagogue. When I went on my own I was ignored because I wasn't seen to 'add value', I had nothing to contribute. I first heard of Reform Judaism through the Jewish feminist movement. There I found strong, capable, articulate women who were Jewishly knowledgeable as well; they had something to say and were listened to. Their talk about struggles in their communities gave me a different perspective on how women could be within Judaism.

Getting involved in a more informal Jewish group took me back to my religious roots and gave me a space to explore what Judaism means to me. I have now had experience of leading services, which is completely scary and completely satisfying. Once you've experienced reading from the Torah scroll you can only feel deprived not to have it. As an Orthodox woman you are usually so far away from the action that you never get to feel that electrifying power.

At heart, though, I don't feel like a Reform Jew, and in fact am currently engaged to marry a man much more religiously observant than myself. Going back into the gallery, at his synagogue, feels strange (see Source I). I wonder about how I will be able to make links with Orthodox women who have lived more conventional lives than mine. The engagement is a personal journey for me as we explore where we might stand on issues from kashrut (food laws) to clothing to theology. For him, it's black and white: personal interpretation is not relevant. Whereas I've got used to a Reform approach of taking my own views into account.

G

In Reform synagogues men and women can sit together.

From secular to Orthodox

H

I grew up with almost no Jewish education from either home or school. Although my father came from a religious family and did belong to a synagogue, he was disillusioned. Then as a teenager I went to my aunt's house at Passover and experienced for the first time a large and atmospheric SEDER, the ritual festive meal. I was also moved by a visit to Israel.

I was always attracted to religious people – such as the man who became my husband! When I got married I knew nothing and suddenly had to start keeping Shabbat, the dietary laws and ritual purity (see page 46). It was like a crash course. That was eighteen years ago, and I've been learning ever since. I have become more observant, and have taken the family along with me.

We are strictly Orthodox. When I was unmarried, I wore jeans. Now I wear skirts, long sleeves and a sheitl (a wig). I am proud to cover myself up, by dressing modestly. In today's world where everything is on show, it's even more important to cover up. I feel very happy that my husband is the only man to see my hair. Sex should be private between a man and wife.

I feel very strongly that women are not equal to men. If anything, on a religious level, they are superior, because they bear children. We therefore don't need the outward signs of Judaism, such as a tallit and tephilin. Men are more subject to the drives of the body, that's why they have been given these things to do, to remind them about God and the commandments. A woman lives in a constant state of prayer, especially around children. Men have to go to synagogue and say prayers to remind them that there is a God. I don't go to synagogue much, because I don't need to. I pray at home with my daughters.

My journey has taken me back to my roots, to the ways of my Polish grandparents, whose silver Shabbat candlesticks I now use.

Miriam Goldberg (not her real name)

I

In an Orthodox synagogue women sit separately from men, either behind a screen or, as here, in a gallery.

(see page 46)

FOCUS TASK

In Sources F and H, Lydia and Miriam describe experiences that affected them.

1 **Copy and complete this table:**

	Things that made me feel valued	Things that made me feel devalued
Lydia		
Miriam		

2 **How do you think Miriam and Lydia would react to the following statements:**
   a) in Judaism men and women are different
   b) in Judaism men and women are equal?

3 **Now use your answers to questions 1 and 2 to role play a discussion between two people, one who thinks Judaism does discriminate against women, another who thinks it doesn't.**

4 **Record your own views on this issue, showing you have considered another point of view.**

3.3 How do Jews respond to racism?

Prejudice and discrimination

- PREJUDICE is an attitude. It means having an opinion which is not based on fact. For example, 'I think he won't do this job well because he is Jewish.'
- DISCRIMINATION is an action. It means treating someone unfairly because of prejudice. For example, 'I won't employ him because he is Jewish.'

In Britain today, racial discrimination is illegal under the 1976 Race Relations Act. However, racial prejudice is not against the law, because an attitude cannot be made illegal.

Personal racism is name-calling, abuse, discrimination, harassment and violence by an individual towards another individual or group.

Institutional racism describes the way that organisations or institutions can develop customs and ways of doing things that exclude or disadvantage people on the basis of race. These habits become ingrained in that organisation's way of working, even if individuals in that organisation would deny they are racist. Sometimes it is hard to spot institutional racism because people take it for granted.

Both types spring from the belief that one group of people is superior to another, thereby justifying the unfair treatment.

ANTI-SEMITISM means prejudice or discrimination specifically against Jews. For the purposes of the 1976 Act, Jews are regarded as a racial group.

ACTIVITY A

1 In pairs, look at the pictures above. Each shows a situation that you or your friends might encounter.
2 In each case, decide in what way and by whom prejudice or discrimination is being shown.
3 Discuss how you feel personally about each case. Could anything be done to improve each situation? By whom?

ACTIVITY B

Jewish teachings on racism can be summed up in five basic principles (right):

1 Copy the five principles on the right into the centre of a page in your notebook.
2 Read each of the quotations in Source A.
3 With a partner, discuss which of these principles each quotation demonstrates.
4 Write out or summarise the quotation next to the principle it demonstrates.

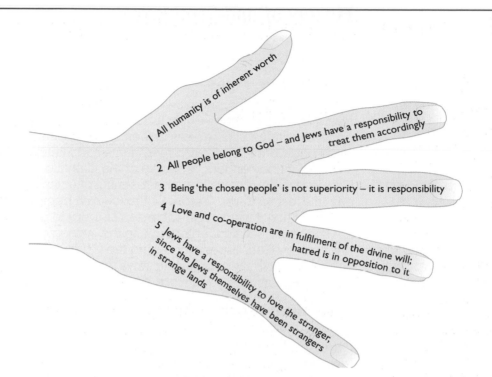

1 All humanity is of inherent worth

2 All people belong to God – and Jews have a responsibility to treat them accordingly

3 Being 'the chosen people' is not superiority – it is responsibility

4 Love and co-operation are in fulfilment of the divine will; hatred is in opposition to it

5 Jews have a responsibility to love the stranger, since the Jews themselves have been strangers in strange lands

A

Love your fellow as yourself.
Leviticus 19.18

I created you, and appointed you a covenant people, a light of nations – opening eyes deprived of light, rescuing prisoners from confinement, from the dungeon those who sit in darkness.
Isaiah 42.6–7

Have we not all one Father? Did not one God create us?
Malachi 2.10

How good and how pleasant it is that brothers dwell together.
Psalm 133.1

And God said, 'Let us make man in our image, after our likeness.'
Genesis 1.26

When a stranger resides with you in your land, you shall not wrong him. The stranger who resides with you shall be to you as one of your citizens; you shall love him as yourself, for you were strangers in the land of Egypt: I the Lord am your God.
Leviticus 19.33–4

Man was created single for the sake of peace among people, so that no one might say to his fellow, 'My father was greater than yours.'
Mishnah Sanhedrin 4.5

Love your neighbour as yourself. That is the whole Torah. All the rest is commentary. Go and learn!
Hillel

Justice, justice shall you pursue.
Deuteronomy 16.20

Blessed be My people Egypt, My handiwork Assyria, and My very own Israel.
Isaiah 19.25

B

A Jew and his secretary were sitting in a coffeehouse in Berlin in 1935. 'Herr Altmann,' said his secretary. 'I notice you're reading Der Sturmer*! I can't understand why you're carrying a Nazi libel sheet. Are you some kind of masochist, or, God forbid, a self-hating Jew?'*

'On the contrary, Frau Epstein. When I used to read the Jewish papers, all I learned about were pogroms, riots in Palestine, and ASSIMILATION *in America. But now that I read* Der Sturmer, *I see that the Jews control all the banks, that we dominate in the arts, and that we're on the verge of taking over the entire world. You know – it makes me feel a whole lot better!'*

From *The Big Book of Jewish Humor*

---

1 **The joke in Source B makes Nazi propaganda look silly. How does it do this?**
2 **Why do you think people make jokes about such serious situations?**

History of anti-Semitism

Despite periods of tolerance and peaceful coexistence, Jews in Europe have often suffered discrimination, forced segregation, attacks, murder and expulsion.

The Middle Ages

European Jewish communities in the Middle Ages were under the control of local rulers and the Catholic Church. Though the Church was hostile to the Jews, rulers generally wanted some Jews in their lands because they were useful. Most Jews were poor, but a few Jewish merchants had international trade links. Some also acted as moneylenders, a trade that the Catholic Church forbade to Christians. Non-Jewish merchants became resentful of Jewish competition and the need to pay interest on loans. Gradually the Church became more powerful than the local rulers. At first it tried persuasion and bribery to get Jews to convert. When this did not succeed, it turned a blind eye to the spread of violence, in which thousands of Jews were killed, especially during the Crusades.

The first country to banish its Jews was England, in 1290. During the next two and a half centuries, Jews were expelled from most countries in western Europe.

The nineteenth century

Jews emigrated towards the East – Poland and Russia – living apart from Christians, as demanded by the Church. During the nineteenth century, Russian Jews were permitted to live only in 'the Pale of Settlement' (which included eastern Poland, Lithuania and Ukraine) and to practise only a few occupations. Resentment against Jews spread from Austria-Hungary and Germany to France and Russia, where serious POGROMS (Russian for 'devastation') broke out from 1881 in reaction to an assassination attempt on the Tsar, Alexander II. In response to these waves of killings, two and a half million Jews left Russia for America.

The twentieth century – the Shoah

In Germany in the 1930s, the Nazis' anti-Semitic policies affected every area of life for Jews and propaganda encouraged anti-Semitism in the German population. As the Nazis took over Europe in the Second World War, they attempted to destroy European Jewry. The large-scale murder that took place between 1941 and 1945 is generally known as the Holocaust, a Greek word meaning 'completely burnt offering'. Jews themselves tend to refer to it as the Shoah, a Hebrew word meaning 'whirlwind' and used in the Tenakh to refer to widespread devastation. It was the culmination of centuries of European anti-Semitic thought and persecution.

21st-century Britain

Jews in Britain today are mostly white, so they can 'blend in'. Yet, anti-Semitism still exists. About 220 incidents are reported each year in Britain.

C

1996	Attempt to push a Jewish schoolgirl under a moving bus
	Jewish man seriously assaulted in Essex, left with broken cheekbone
	Desecration of Jewish cemeteries in Glasgow and Edinburgh
1997	Hit-and-run attempts by car drivers against synagogue-goers
	Air rifle shootings of rabbi and congregants in Muswell Hill, London
1998	Pig's head left on doorstep of synagogue in Salford
	Three explicit bomb threats against Jewish buildings – all hoaxes
2000	Jewish man stabbed on a bus in East London

Some anti-Semitic incidents in the UK

D

People usually hate what they do not understand.
Moses Ibn Ezra (1060 – 1138)

SAVE AS...

Write three short paragraphs:

1 **What benefits did Jews bring to the countries in which they lived?**

2 **Why did the Church encourage anti-Semitism?**

3 **Why did ordinary people resent Jews?**

DISCUSS

1 **Look at Sources E and F. What do these two scenes have in common?**

2 **What would be the best response to each? Give reasons.**

<u>W</u>hy have Jews experienced such hostility from their neighbours?

1 **Christianity** – the Catholic Church in the past encouraged anti-Judaism by teaching false ideas, such as that the Jews were responsible for the killing of Christ. Anti-Jewish riots used to be common at Easter. Jews were also falsely accused of killing Christian children to make MATZAH (unleavened bread for Passover) with their blood, and of poisoning wells. The Church taught that the Jews deserved to be punished for their rejection of the 'truth' of Christianity.

2 **Economics** – the success of some Jews as moneylenders in medieval times, and later as merchants, caused resentment. The poor, particularly in eastern Europe, often identified Jews with the rulers on whose behalf Jews collected taxes or ran estates. Anti-Semitic literature of that time portrays Jews as secretly planning to take over the economy and governments of the whole world.

3 **Racial theories** – anthropologists in the mid-nineteenth century divided human beings into races characterised by physical features such as head shape, skin colour and body measurements. The scientists also developed racist views that certain physical features were superior or more desirable. This 'science' fed racism. Whites were held to have superior features, and Jews inferior. Anti-Semitism became part of European culture in the second half of the nineteenth century and prepared the ground for Nazism.

In addition, throughout history human beings have feared people different from themselves and people often hate what they fear.

E

In Nazi Germany, anti-Semitic policies forbade Jews from entering shops.

F

This Jewish cemetery in Britain was vandalised and daubed with graffiti in 1999.

How have Jews responded to anti-Semitism?

A millennium of anti-Semitism and persecution has taken its toll on Jews as a group and individually. Many Jews, in Israel and the diaspora, have grown up assuming that the rest of the world harbours hostility towards them. Even if they personally do not experience anti-Semitism, it is felt to lurk just beneath the surface. This has led to a range of responses.

Turning inward
Some Jews have isolated themselves from non-Jews. They focus their efforts on the Jewish community.

Celebrating multiculturalism
Some Jews have tried to make Jews and Judaism a thoroughly integrated part of modern multicultural society, but without losing or compromising Judaism.

Supporting the persecuted
For some Jews, the experience of persecution has created a positive resolve to support others suffering racism.

RESPONSES TO ANTI-SEMITISM

Rejecting Judaism
For some Jews the response has been to turn away from Judaism. For them anything Jewish is almost totally negative, since it has always seemed to lead to discrimination and persecution.

Suspicion of non-Jews
Some Jews still fear those who have persecuted them. Those who lived through the Shoah, and their children, often remain wary of those responsible for that genocide.

Protecting the Jewish community
As you read on page 58, anti-Semitism does exist today. Incidents include extreme violence, assault, damage to property, abusive behaviour and threats. Some Jews take action to protect the Jewish community from such attacks.

SAVE AS...
Record your own simplified version of these responses.

G

I grew up with very conflicting feelings about being Jewish. I hated my parents for being Jews and thereby making me Jewish. Particularly, they were the kind of 'Jewish' it was impossible to hide. On the one hand, as a schoolgirl, I was critical that they were not religious enough, and on the other I envied my Jewish friends their professional, South African-born parents, with their ease, their education, and their ability to be inconspicuous. Later on, I put my energy into dissociating myself from Judaism and the Jewish community.

Margaret is the daughter of Holocaust survivors. She grew up in South Africa.

H

A young Talmud scholar who left Poland for America returns several years later to visit his family.
'But where is your beard?' asks his mother.
'Mama, in America nobody wears a beard.'
'But at least you keep the Sabbath?'
'Mama, business is business. In America people work on the Sabbath.'
'But kosher food you still eat?'
'Mama, it's very difficult to keep kosher in America.'
The old lady hesitates for a moment, and whispers, 'Son, tell me one thing, Are you still circumcised?'

From *The Big Book of Jewish Humor*

I

The Community Security Trust (CST) provides security advice and services to the Jewish community in Britain. Working alongside the police, it researches and aims to counter racism, anti-Semitism and terrorism. The CST provides training in security and self-defence to Jewish organisations and individuals. About 2000 volunteers can be called on to guard Jewish communal events, assist the police, and monitor the activities of the extreme Right and other anti-Semitic activists, including those active on the Internet.

DISCUSS

Look at Sources G–L.
1. **Match each source to a response on page 60. You may feel some show more than one response.**
2. **Which responses are:**
   a) positive, and likely to reduce racism
   b) negative, and likely to increase racism?
   Give reasons.
3. **Do you think any of the responses are themselves racist?**
4. **Look back to page 57.**
   a) Which responses are most consistent with the principles of Judaism?
   b) Which are least consistent?
   Give reasons.
5. **Which response is the most understandable? Give reasons.**

J

Three generations ago my great-grandparents, like many other Jews, came as refugees to this country, so I feel I have a moral obligation to help those in similar situations. Since training as a lawyer I have always wanted to work in legal aid to help those at the bottom of the pile, and make a difference to their lives. I come from a family of left-wing Jews, and all of us have chosen work in some area of social justice.

Jessica Wyman is a solicitor. She helps immigrants who are here illegally, or who want to stay because of marriage, with their applications for asylum.

K

To me they are all guilty, whether they are the perpetrators or the next generation. Neo-Nazis are thriving all over Europe, not just in Germany, and it's always possible that the Hitler times might repeat themselves. I can only visit Germany today – to visit relatives – by denying to myself that I'm there. I used to look at Germans over a certain age and guess at what they were doing during the war. These days, I think of the young people as probably being the children of Nazis. Having lived through those times, I am pessimistic. I can't believe that there would be a complete change and that young people in Germany or Poland would suddenly become pro-Jewish or pro-Israeli. The Poles have been anti-Semites for years and years.

Beata Kreisler (not her real name) is a Jewish woman who as a teenager spent three years during the war living in hiding in Hungary.

L

The tendency to be suspicious of those who are different is one we usually contain, but which can sometimes erupt out of control and spiral downwards into fear, resentment and hostility . . . The religious response must be to try to help people to see themselves in others and accept that variations in colour, creed and custom should not blind us to shared hopes, emotions and pricked hands. It should encourage us to regard others as possible friends and to view differences as enriching.

From 'The Nazi that lurks within us' by Rabbi Jonathan Romain, *The Times*, 28 November 1992

'Protect the alien and the stranger'

M

It seems to me that true religion begins with the law about protecting and shielding the alien and the stranger . . . How you are with the one to whom you owe nothing, that is a grave test and not only as an index of our tragic past. I always think that the real offenders at the halfway mark of the century were the bystanders, all those people who let things happen because it didn't affect them directly.

Rabbi Hugo Gryn (1930–96) was sent to Auschwitz with his family in 1944. He survived and went on to become a leading Reform rabbi in Britain. Through regular radio appearances he was well known as a spokesperson for tolerance and understanding between all people.

ACTIVITY A

Read Dr Friedman's comments in Source O. Write two paragraphs on:

a) what motivates her in her work

b) what Jewish teachings from page 57 might inspire her.

The Jewish Council for Racial Equality (J-CORE)

J-CORE is a Jewish organisation that works to counteract racism in all areas of British society. Some of J-CORE's projects include:

- giving practical aid to refugees to the UK, and campaigning to influence the government's legislation on refugees and asylum-seekers
- providing career support and retraining to refugee doctors and lawyers
- promoting Black/Jewish/Asian dialogue through a breakfast discussion forum, writing letters to the press, and a schools' exhibition on the relationship between these three groups
- developing materials for anti-racist education in, especially, Jewish schools.

N

Help us to create a more just and equal society...

For Black, Asian and other ethnic minorities in the UK, discrimination, harassment and violent attacks are an everyday occurrence.

As Jews we also know the consequences of racism only too well. We know the consequences when others stand by and do nothing. Our community needs to speak out in support of those who today are suffering racism. As Jews we can help to bring about change and challenge racism at its roots.

This is why the Jewish Council for Racial Equality was set up in 1976. It works to bring people from Asian, Black and Jewish communities together in projects which aim to combat prejudice and racism and promote equal opportunities for all in Britain's multi-racial society.

It is a non-political organisation which receives the backing of religious and secular leaders.

The aims of J-CORE are:

- To raise awareness amongst the Jewish community of the need for racial equality
- To encourage and stimulate the Jewish community to take an active role in promoting racial equality
- To foster close and co-operative relations with other minority groups and race equality groups, taking joint action where appropriate
- To support initiatives and campaigns which challenge racism

O

I was bemused at constantly hearing Christians quote the Jewish prophets. I wanted to hear Jews do this, to reclaim their tradition of social activism. It's important that all of us are aware of other traditions and faiths so that no one can feel they have a monopoly on ethics.

The British-Jewish community is closer to the Holocaust experience than Jews in the USA, where I come from. In America so many people belong to minority groups, but in Britain Jews sometimes feel vulnerable and uneasy taking on the outside world. They may feel that in what is perceived to be a Christian country their voices are not always heard. Despite this, in Britain as well as in other countries such as the USA and South Africa, individual Jews are disproportionately involved in human rights organising.

My vision for J-CORE was that individuals and communities should see the work of building a more economically and socially just society as part and parcel of what it means to be Jewish. It's actually one's responsibility in being human, as expressed in Jewish teaching. A plural, open society is one that's healthy for all of us.

The Jewish Council for Racial Equality (J-CORE) was set up by Dr Edie Friedman in 1976. She wanted to increase the Jewish community's involvement in a wide range of campaigns, including anti-racism.

ACTIVITY B

Read Source P. Imagine
you are the Reverend
Faith Whitmore.

1 **What might she have
said in her speech?**
2 **What might the rabbi
have said in response?**

Nothing in my life prepared me for this!

In 1999 a synagogue in California, USA was firebombed by racist attackers.
Source P describes what happened next.

P

I have been a member of Congregation B'nai Israel for the past 17 years. This is our 150th anniversary. We are the oldest congregation west of the Mississippi.

Immediately after the attack, members of our temple (synagogue) phoned each other seeking news about how bad it really was, since we were not allowed anywhere near the site. Was this the beginning of another reign of terror for us? How could this happen in America? What have we done? Why do they hate us so much? All we ask is that we be allowed to live in peace and safety within the dominant Christian community.

We heard that our Friday service would be held in the 2000-seat Community Theatre. I figured that there

The library at the synagogue was completely gutted.

would be enough people there to fill up a few rows. When I arrived I was totally surprised. Eighteen hundred people from all over our community, Jews, Catholics, Buddhists, Hare Krishnas, and members from every sect of the Protestant community were there. There were members from black churches, gay churches, Asian churches, as well as atheists, agnostics, and some of the followers of so-called 'new age' spiritual leaders. There were ministers, bishops, city council members, the police chief, and representatives from the state legislature and governor's office. Never have I seen such an outpouring of grief and concern from the community . . . for Jews.

There were a number of speakers from our congregation and from the community. Then something happened that I will never forget. Our rabbi said he wanted to introduce us to a Rev. Faith Whitmore, a leader of the United Methodist Church. She got up and spoke briefly about how appalled she was about these incidents. We've heard it before. From the Pope on down, all through the years its been 'Gee, sorry for the Holocaust but there's nothing I could have done about it.'

She took out a piece of paper. 'This afternoon we took a special collection from our members to help you rebuild your temple and we want you to have this cheque for six thousand dollars.' For two seconds there was absolute quiet. We were astounded. Did we hear this correctly? Christians are going to do this? On the third second the hall shook with a thunderous applause. And it went on for two minutes. And then people broke into tears. It was like all of the emotion of the day and evening poured out in those few minutes. Those in my parents' generation were dumbfounded. Who ever heard of Gentiles caring about Jews?

As Rev. Whitmore gave the cheque to the rabbi and hugged him, it was one of the most emotional moments I've ever been witness to. In my entire lifetime I've never known an organised Christian denomination to officially do anything 'nice' for a Jewish congregation. Our congregation, some 1100 of us, stood with tears in our eyes. Christians who for centuries sent the Cossacks to pillage our towns, who put us through their Inquisitions, who burned us at the stake as heretics, who expelled us from their countries, who locked us away in ghettos, who eagerly turned us in to the Nazi SS, and who ran the trains, who produced the poison gas, or just 'knew' about the greatest human tragedy of this century . . . were doing something good for a Jew. Nothing in my life prepared me for that.

From an article on the Internet by Alan N. Canton, Vice-President, Congregation B'nai Israel

FOCUS TASK

**Imagine you are a
member of the social
action committee of a
synagogue. The
committee wants to help
a poor immigrant family
who have recently
moved to this country.
They want the
community to provide
practical and financial
support.**

**Write an article for
the synagogue magazine
explaining why the whole
community should
support this plan. You
will need to include:**

- **what Jewish teachings
  say about
  responsibilities to the
  'stranger'**
- **what Jews have learned
  from their history
  about helping others**
- **how each individual can
  play their part.**

3.4 How can individuals change society?

ACTIVITY
1 Read Source A. What might a modern-day Isaiah criticise in our society, and what demands would he make? Write a short speech for him.
2 Write your response to his demands, explaining how they could be carried out.

Jews have been on the move since Biblical times, when Abraham was told by God to go 'from your native land . . . to the land that I will show you.' (Genesis 12.1). From the time of their first expulsion – from England in 1290 – up until the present day, persecution and the search for a better life have led many Jews to start new lives in strange countries.

Jewish teachings require one to respect the laws of the land where one lives. This concept is known as 'derech eretz' (the way of the land). The Talmud states that 'The law of the land is the law' (Baba Kamma 113a). In making this ruling, the rabbis insisted that, in matters of criminal and civil law, Jews had to follow the rules of the country in which they lived, so traditionally Jews have been law-abiding citizens who try not to 'rock the boat' and accept the way the world is.

However, there is another strong tradition within Judaism – the prophetic tradition. This calls on people to protest against injustice and to work to make this world a better place. The belief in right over might stems from the Torah. The Prophets often pointed to the hypocrisy of those people, especially rulers, who presented themselves as religious while exploiting their fellow human beings.

Teachings from Jewish texts

For over a thousand years the Torah and the Talmud have offered Jews guidance on how to live. They place a strong emphasis on justice, compassion and kindness. They insist on service to others, even at the expense of a person's own convenience or self-interest. It is a duty to offer hospitality to strangers, visit the sick, comfort mourners and return lost objects to their rightful owners. Indeed, if a life is at risk, all laws except murder, idolatry, incest and adultery must be suspended.

A

This is the fast I desire:
To unlock fetters of
*   wickedness,*
And untie the cords of the
*   yoke*
To let the oppressed go
*   free;*
To break off every yoke.
It is to share your bread
*   with the hungry,*
And to take the wretched
*   poor into your home;*
When you see the naked,
*   to clothe him,*
And not to ignore your
*   own kin.*

Isaiah 58.6–7

B

Rabbi Akiva once visited a disciple who had become ill. No one else had bothered to visit the student. As a result of his illness – and the fact that nobody had come to visit or offer help – the student's house was a mess. Rabbi Akiva rolled up his sleeves and got to work. He even swept the man's floors. When his student recovered, he attributed his restored health to Rabbi Akiva's visit. Akiva then went out and taught: 'One who does not visit the sick is like someone who sheds blood.' Rabbi Dimi added, 'One who visits the sick causes them to recover; one who does not visit the sick causes that person to die.'

Talmud, Nedarim 40a

C

On the Day of Judgement, everyone will be asked, 'What was your occupation?'

If the person answers, 'I used to feed the hungry,' they will say to that person, 'This is God's gate; you who fed the hungry may enter.'

If the person answers, 'I used to give water to those who were thirsty,' they will say to that person, 'This is God's gate; you who gave water to the thirsty may enter.'

If the person answers, 'I used to clothe the naked,' they will say to that person, 'This is God's gate; you who clothed the naked may enter.'

And similarly with those who raised orphans, and those who performed the mitzvah of charity and those who performed acts of compassion and kindness.

Midrash, Tehillim 118:17

Case study – Avodah: The Jewish Service Corps

What should a Jew do who wants to contribute to society? There are of course many choices, but one specifically Jewish one started recently in the USA. Avodah was launched in 1998 by Rabbi David Rosenn. He was inspired to set up the programme by seeing the success of similar organisations within other religions. At that time there seemed to him to be a lack of meaningful opportunities in the Jewish world for social activism.

In Hebrew, the word 'avodah' means three things: work, worship and religious service. Avodah is a programme that places young Jewish college graduates in a social service or social justice organisation for a year of low-paying work, combined with a year of intensive Jewish study.

They work with the homeless, with disadvantaged foster children and immigrants, in AIDS day-treatment centres, and run after-school programmes (see Source D).

Participants (called 'Avodahniks') share a household and are paired up with professional and spiritual mentors.

Avodah emphasises the link between social activism and Jewish tradition. For example, examining Jewish sources on the elderly may be followed by delivering food packages to home-bound old people.

Avodah has a website that is frequently updated (www.avodah.net/). As well as details of the projects and participants, it also features teachings on Judaism and social justice.

D

Avodahnik Brian Fink with a client at the Urban Justice Center. He helps people who are having problems with their benefits.

Avodahniks with Abby Rosin of 'Groove with me'. This organisation helps at-risk teenage girls through dance and movement training.

There are so many Jews involved in social change work, but so few of them connect that work to their Jewish life. I couldn't find any Jews who said to me that their involvement in the Jewish community sustained them. That seemed to me a problem.

Rabbi David Rosenn, founder and director of Avodah

I think there are young Jewish adults who see the connection between Jewish identity and a commitment to justice as seamless. This is such a natural fit. This is where our tradition is.

Elizabeth Greenstein works for one of Avodah's funding organisations.

Avodahniks discuss a community mural with Americorps staff in Red Hook, Brooklyn.

Avodahnik Elizabeth Lamin helps clients at the West Side Campaign Against Hunger.

Relationships – Review tasks

A

1 On a scale of 1 to 5 (1 is low, 5 is high) rate how important the family is within Judaism. Explain your score carefully.

2 Give two practical examples to show how the practices and teachings of Judaism strengthen family life.

3 Describe two contrasting views from within Judaism on the role of a Jewish woman.

4 'There's more to being a Jewish family than eating together!'

Explain how far you agree or disagree with this statement, showing that you have considered other points of view.

B

1 Explain the difference between prejudice and discrimination using examples drawn from Judaism.

2 Outline at least two teachings from the Torah that Jews might use to oppose prejudice and discrimination.

3 Describe three different Jewish responses to anti-Semitism.

4 'When you suffer discrimination yourself, you are more likely to help someone else who suffers too.'

Do you agree? In your answer you must show that you have considered other points of view. Make sure you illustrate your answer with examples from Judaism.

UNIT 4

Global issues

What do you think would be a good caption for this picture?

Over the next twenty-five pages, you will be investigating some big issues: poverty, the environment, war and peace. Here are some even bigger questions to think about before you start.

Do you feel that the Earth belongs:
- to you
  - to someone else
    - to no one
      - to God?

Do you feel that solving the major global problems is:
- your responsibility
  - other people's responsibility
    - God's responsibility?

Do you feel the biggest threat to life on Earth is:
- poverty
  - environmental change
    - war
      - something else?

If someone said to you that religion can help solve the Earth's problems, would you:
- agree
  - disagree
    - scream?

4.1 How should Jews use their money?

DISCUSS

1 Do you agree with the classification in Source A?
2 Which character are you closest to?
3 Which would you like to be closest to?
4 Do you think sayings like this are helpful in real life?

A

One who says, 'Mine is mine and yours is yours' is an average person, though some say he is [callous] or [selfish].

One who says, 'Mine is yours and yours is mine' is a foolish person.

One who says, 'Mine is yours and yours is yours' is a saint.

One who says, 'Yours is mine and mine is mine' is a wicked person.

From Ethics of the Fathers

B

Tzedakah boxes are found in synagogues and in many Jewish homes. It is customary to give some money every day, except for Shabbat and Jewish holidays when handling money is not allowed.

re Jews obliged to give?

Judaism teaches that humans are custodians, not owners, of wealth. However much or little money Jews own or earn, they are obliged by their religion to use it to help those poorer than themselves. They cannot choose whether or not to give. The Hebrew word for this is TZEDAKAH. This word has no direct equivalent in English, but it roughly means 'doing righteous acts'. It is every Jew's obligation to act by giving money, goods or time to make the world a better place and to relieve human suffering. Tzedakah is given individually, by a family or communally.

Tzedakah was originally like a form of tax. Typically it was set at 10 per cent of income; 20 per cent was the maximum permissible. Giving even a small amount, though, was and is acceptable.

C

When you reap the harvest of your land, you shall not reap all the way to the edges of your field, or gather the gleanings of your harvest. You shall not pick your vineyard bare, or gather the fallen fruit of your vineyard. You shall leave them for the poor and the stranger. I the Lord am your God.

Leviticus 19.9–10

1 Look at Source C. What might be a modern equivalent of this commandment?

2 Look at Source H. Find five things Isaiah says people should do and list them using your own words.

3 In pairs discuss the advantages and disadvantages of setting maximum and minimum amounts for giving.

4 Read the views in Source G on ways of giving tzedekah. Which one appeals most to you? Explain your choice.

D

Open your hand to the poor and your neighbours in your land who are in need.

Deuteronomy 15.11

E

a) *Poverty is like death.*

Talmud, Nedarim 64b

b) *Tzedakah saves from death.*

Talmud, Bava Batra 10a

F

Even a person who lives on tzedakah should practice tzedakah.

Talmud, Gittin 7b

G

I have set up a couple of standing orders from my bank account. Each month ten pounds goes automatically to World Jewish Relief and ten pounds to The British Heart Foundation.

At the end of the month, our family sits down together and goes through all the charity appeals that have been sent to us in the post. We have allocated thirty pounds for our monthly tzedakah and each month we choose a different charity.

I am an osteopath, and every week I spend one afternoon giving my services free to patients who can't afford the cost of treatment.

Our synagogue runs a tzedakah collective. We all pay five per cent of our income into it through our banks. Twice a year we all meet to discuss which charities we should support for the next six months.

My wife and I don't support any particular charities regularly. We just give if someone rattles a can at us.

H

This is the fast I desire:
To unlock fetters of
wickedness,
And untie the cords of the
yoke,
To let the oppressed go
free;
To break off every yoke.
It is to share your food
with the hungry,
And to take the wretched
poor into your home;
When you see the naked,
to clothe him,
And not to ignore your
own kin.

Isaiah 58.6–7

SAVE AS...

1 Write a label to go on the box in Source B explaining why people should give generously. Use the information and quotations on these two pages to help you.

What is the best way of giving?

Principle 1: How you give matters!

Rabbi Moses Ben Maimon, known as Maimonides, was a philosopher, Talmud-scholar and physician who lived in Spain and Egypt in the twelfth century. He wrote the Mishneh Torah, a code of Jewish law that to this day remains influential in Jewish thinking (see page 98). In discussing the laws of gifts to the poor, he described eight 'levels' of tzedakah.

I

1. Gives to help a person become self-sufficient

2. The giver does not know the receiver and the receiver does not know who gave

3. The giver knows the receiver, but the receiver does not know who gave

4. The giver does not know the receiver, but the receiver knows who gave

5. Gives directly to a person in need, before being asked

6. Gives directly to a person in need, after being asked

7. Gives directly to a person in need, cheerfully, but should give more

8. Gives a small amount reluctantly, with a scowl

Principle 2: Who you give to matters!

Within Jewish communities, charity traditionally began at home. At early times in history tzedakah went to support the priests who served in the Temple in Jerusalem, then – after the destruction of the Temple – students of Torah, as well as the poor. Source J shows the traditional order of priorities.

However, Jews are also required to help those of other religions or cultures.

J

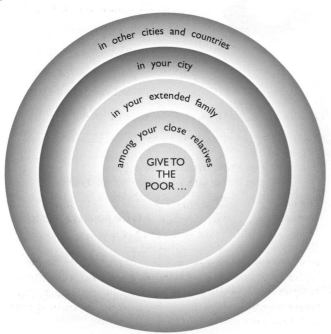

in other cities and countries

in your city

in your extended family

among your close relatives

GIVE TO THE POOR ...

K

Poor Gentiles should be supported as well as poor Jews; the Gentile sick should be visited as well as the Jewish sick; and their dead should be buried as well as the Jewish dead, for the sake of good peaceful relations.

Talmud, Gittin 61a

> ## DISCUSS
>
> 1 Look at Source J. What is the reason for this order of priorities?
> 2 Does Source K agree with these priorities?
> 3 Do you agree with the order in Source J? Give reasons for and against.

L

How do I know you won't spend it on a massage?

The shnorrer

A well-loved character in Jewish humour is the 'shnorrer', a cheeky Jewish beggar who considers that being given tzedakah is his right – which in Jewish law of course it is. He treats the rich man's money as his own. There are many jokes and funny stories about shnorrers.

N

Mrs Krasnov, feeling sorry for a shnorrer who appeared at her door, invited him in and gave him a substantial meal: chicken, kugel (noodle-pudding), wine, and two kinds of bread: black bread and challah (soft white bread).

The shnorrer devoured everything he was given, except the black bread. 'The challah was wonderful,' he said. 'Do you have any more?'

'My dear man,' said Mrs Krasnov, 'We have plenty of black bread, but challah is very expensive.'

'I know,' said the shnorrer. 'But believe me, lady, it's worth it!'

From *The Big Book of Jewish Humor*

I Read Source N. What does the joke tell you about:
a) the attitude of the shnorrer
b) the attitude of Mrs Krasnov?

How should Jews respond to beggars?

The problem of homeless people begging on the streets has prompted some Jews to consider what tzedakah means to them. Arthur Kurzweil, Editor-in-Chief of Jason Aronson Publishers, noticed that his response to 'beggars' depended on his own mood and the impression made by the person asking for help. He wrote a list of fifteen questions (see Save As . . .) to help himself sort out a more consistent way of responding, and then tried to find Jewish teachings that helped with the answers. He says he struggles to live up to the teachings, but that it is important to try.

M

a) *Rabbi Shmelke of Nicholsburg said, 'When a poor man asks for aid, do not use his faults as an excuse for not helping him.'*

Unzer Alter Otzer II p.99

b) *Nehemiah of Sihin met a man in Jerusalem who said to him, 'Give me that chicken you are carrying.' Nehemiah said, 'Here is its value in money.' The man went and bought some meat and ate it and died. Then Nehemiah said, 'Come and bemoan the man whom Nehemiah has killed.'*

Jerusalem Talmud, Pe'ah 8.9

c) *Although the poor are everywhere supported from the communal chest, if they wish in addition to beg from door to door they may do so, and each should give according to his understanding and desire.*

Responsa of Solomon ben Adret III: 380

SAVE AS . . .

Here are some of Arthur Kurzweil's questions:

- **Should I leave official organisations to support these people?**
- **Should I give them food or money?**
- **Should I give if they are obviously alcoholics?**

1 Draw up a table with three columns. In the first column copy out his questions. Now read Source M. In the second column write the letter of the text in Source M that helps to answer each question.
2 In the third column write a possible answer to each question applying the text to modern life.
3 Do you think religious teachings about money are ideals or achievable? Explain your answer, showing that you have considered other points of view.

Giving to Jews: World Jewish Relief

World Jewish Relief was set up to save Jewish lives. It began in 1933 by funding and organising the Kindertransport, which brought 10,000 Jewish children from Nazi Germany to Britain. Since then it has specialised in providing discreet assistance to Jews in politically sensitive areas in Europe, the Middle East and Africa. For example, it rescued more than 2000 Jews from war-torn Sarajevo in the former Yugoslavia, and funded preparations for the airlift of Ethiopian Jews to Israel at a time of famine and civil war. Today it cares for tens of thousands of needy Jews in the former Soviet Union, Bulgaria and former Yugoslavia.

Helping abroad

In the former Soviet Union there are about 2 million Jews, despite a wave of recent immigration to Israel. Half are elderly and, of these, half are desperately poor. Their situation has deteriorated since the end of the Communist era. Any pension they receive is inadequate to pay for the basic necessities of life: food, clothing, warmth and medicines. They often have to choose between eating and staying warm. World Jewish Relief raises money to provide care workers, meals on wheels, medicines and clothing. In the longer term it is planning to build a welfare and community centre in the Ukrainian capital, Kiev. It also provides desperately needed help for the smaller communities in Bulgaria and former Yugoslavia.

O

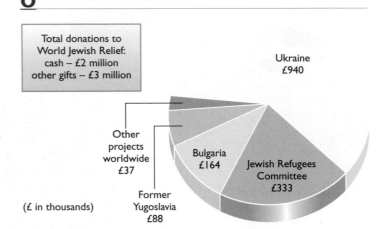

Total donations to World Jewish Relief:
cash – £2 million
other gifts – £3 million

Ukraine £940

Other projects worldwide £37

Bulgaria £164

Jewish Refugees Committee £333

Former Yugoslavia £88

(£ in thousands)

Money spent by World Jewish Relief in 1998. Since the break-up of the Soviet Union, World Jewish Relief has been able to make its work more public. As a result, donations of money and goods have increased by 50 per cent.

P

Some 500,000 elderly Jews in the former Soviet Union live in desperate poverty.

ACTIVITY

You are in charge of advertising and promotion at World Jewish Relief. Design a poster to raise money for elderly Jews in the former Soviet Union (see Source P). Your poster should explain:

- the origins of World Jewish Relief
- its aims
- the reasons Jews should support its work in the former Soviet Union.

Draw up three columns with the headings:

- **Rescue**
- **Refugees**
- **Support in home country.**

In each column give examples of World Jewish Relief's work.

DISCUSS

1 **Look at Source Q. How is World Jewish Relief going to raise money?**
2 **Do you think this is a good way of raising money? Why?**
3 **How has it appealed to people's consciences?**
4 **Do you think it is a good way of appealing to people? Why?**
5 **How is the money going to be spent?**
6 **Do you think this is a good use of the money? Why?**

Helping at home

Britain has also had its share of Jewish refugees, the largest recent wave being before and after the Shoah. Today most Jewish refugees are from the former Communist bloc and from some Arab and Muslim countries. World Jewish Relief offers counselling, advice and practical support.

Q

Remembering the children of yesterday.
Helping the children of today.

You would need a good reason to choose to go to Auschwitz, the place of the darkest moments in Jewish, and indeed human, history.

We're going there to remember the victims of the Holocaust, to commemorate the escape of thousands of Jewish children on the Kindertransport, and to help tens of thousands of Jewish children who today are in great need in the former Soviet Union.

We are organising a sponsored bike ride from 24th June - 1st July 2001. It starts at the Brandenburg Gate in Berlin and ends at the gates of Auschwitz,

a journey of 500 kilometres. Proceeds from the bike ride will be split between two projects: supporting children's projects in the former Soviet Union, and creating a new commemorative sculpture to the Kindertransport.

We believe it will be a moving and very rewarding journey. **For more information, please contact Rutti Goldberger on 020-7691 1775 or email rg@wjr.org.uk.**

A World Jewish Relief fundraising poster

TZEDEK
JEWISH ACTION FOR A JUST WORLD

Giving to others: Tzedek – Jewish action for a just world

The Jewish charity Tzedek was founded in 1990. It was inspired by the traditional idea that Jews should be 'a light to the world' and should work to make the world a better place. Working with some of the world's poorest communities, regardless of race or religion, it aims to help them become self-sufficient.

Tzedek's work falls into two main areas:

- relieving and eliminating poverty in the developing world by providing direct support for sustainable self-help programmes
- educating the Jewish community about the causes and effects of poverty and the Jewish obligation to respond.

Practical work in the developing world

Tzedek works primarily in India and Africa. It sends funds, and also volunteers: young people who spend two or more months working with specific non-governmental projects. Its programmes in India include sponsoring street-children in Calcutta through an income-generating training scheme and providing start-up finance to women's self-help schemes in the state of Tamil Nadu. In Zimbabwe volunteers work with such organisations as the Abandoned Babies Committee and Inter-Country People's Aid.

R

Spiti is a very desolate area of India, and largely inaccessible due to its location in the Himalayas near Tibet. I went there because I wanted to do something useful in my year off before my degree. Educational facilities are non-existent, because no Indian teachers can be tempted to live in an area that cannot be left for eleven months of the year. If we can help them improve their living conditions, we will in the long-term help a community to support itself through the much needed education of its children.

Melissa Parsons taught English in a remote village school in Spiti in the Indian Himalayas.

1. **Look back at Source I on page 70. On which level of Maimonides' ladder does Tzedek operate?**
2. **The Talmud says, 'The blessing of tzedakah is greater for the person who gives than the person who receives.' (Vayikra Rabbah 34.10) What evidence is there in Sources R and T to support this?**

S

Mealtime at Spiti

T

I'd packed little, and my one t-shirt soon became dusty, torn and smelly, which enhanced my understanding of the minimums my pupils lived by. For the pupils I went out to teach, having both shoes was a luxury; pen and paper an unlikely combination; lunch was an ice-pop. They sit 45 to a class, on low wooden benches, hanging on to every word the teacher says. There is not one textbook, no phone, no office, no lab, no paintbrushes, nothing but a teacher, a board, and suffocating heat. Yet the students I taught were the brightest, most eager, most sincerely hard-working group I've ever had the fortune to meet.

Deborah Levin taught in a school located in a squatter camp near Harare, the capital of Zimbabwe.

Case study: Clive Lawton

Clive Lawton has been headteacher of a large Jewish secondary school in Liverpool and has held several high-profile professional roles in the British Jewish community. He now donates some of his time unpaid to be Chair of Trustees for Tzedek.

U

How did you first learn about tzedakah?

From the time I was very young, my parents brought me up with the principle that I should set aside a tenth of my money for one form or another of charity. Even when I was a student, on very limited income, it was so well drummed into me that I still did it, and continue to do so now. I also watched my parents devote a lot of time to communal and intercommunal work. So I was brought up with the need to allocate both money and time to those less well-off.

What does tzedakah mean to you?

'Charity' is a poor translation of tzedakah, since they are utterly different concepts and come from different cultural roots. The experience of both recipient and donor is different. In Britain the idea of a welfare state has existed for only the last hundred years, but Jews have been constructing their welfare state for centuries, probably millennia. And they continue to provide such services to their poor, regardless of what the state supplies. This trains you up to the concept that the community is a bigger thing than just yourself.

Should Jews be wealthy?

Jewish teaching doesn't say it's wrong to be rich, but does ask you to do good with it. I am proud of how astonishingly generous the Jewish community is. What Jews consider a reasonable contribution would in most parts of British society be considered hugely generous. Most Jews won't even turn down an envelope labelled Christian Aid! A newspaper report recently quoted a successful City businessman, who said that one of the good things about being rich is that you can give your money away! I thought that was a wonderfully Jewish comment. Judaism says you should stand on your own two feet, but you should be concerned about other people. I think that's something society at large still struggles with and can't get right.

Why do you believe in giving to non-Jews?

Judaism holds that all human beings are created in the image of God. Uniquely amongst the major religions, we don't imagine a world in which everybody will eventually be us. Other people are part of God's creation and concern. Isaiah (chapter 19) says God is as interested in the Assyrians and the Egyptians as he is in the Jews.

Tzedek is not the mainstream – understandably. The idea that if Jews don't look after Jews nobody else will is a very potent idea, and therefore understandably the Jewish community cares for Jews. But I've never come across any Jewish audience that doesn't react very positively to the message of Tzedek. So I give Tzedek my time because the job has to be done; because it attracts me as an under-explored area of Jewish responsibility; and because you can't refuse when you are offered a chance to carry out one of God's commandments.

FOCUS TASK

A synagogue has the custom of 'adopting' one charity to support each year.

Imagine your class are members of the synagogue council. You have to choose between **World Jewish Relief** and **Tzedek**. You have the information on pages 72–75 to help you decide, as well as the other information in this chapter.

1 **Split the class into two groups. One group prepare the case for supporting World Jewish Relief. The other group prepare the case for supporting Tzedek.**
2 **Debate the case for each charity and vote on your choice.**
3 **Write an article for the synagogue newsletter explaining to members why they should give generously. Include:**

   • **which charity has been chosen**
   • **what it does**
   • **how its work fits in with Jewish teachings on tzedakah.**

4.2 When the desert is a meadow the Messiah will appear!

Tu B'Shevat – the New Year for trees

Many Jewish festivals have their origin in the natural world or the farming calendar, but one has come to be seen as specifically environmental. Named after the date in the Hebrew calendar on which it falls, the 15th of Shevat, TU B'SHEVAT marks the New Year of the Trees. In the second century CE, it was set as the date for calculating the ages of trees and tithing (taxing) their fruit.

But Tu B'Shevat was not only a tax date. Like humans on Rosh Hashanah (Jewish New Year), on Tu B'Shevat the trees were thought to be judged by God to decide their fruitfulness for the coming year.

The day chosen 1800 years ago for this 'birthday' of the trees was when the rabbis thought the sap began to rise in their roots and trunks as winter moved towards spring. In our Gregorian calendar the 15th of Shevat falls in late January or early February.

Centuries later, in the 1500s, mystical Jewish thinkers known as KABBALISTS brought new life to Tu B'Shevat. They believed that humans shared with God the task of renewing creation every spring. They created a Tu B'Shevat seder (see Source A): a ritual meal accompanied by readings from a HAGGADAH (see Source B). It was modelled on the Passover seder (see page 102). By blessing and eating many fruits, the Kabbalists believed that people could help nature be reborn after the winter. Since the sixteenth century, more and more Jews throughout the world have adopted the practice of holding a Tu B'Shevat seder, although it is not nearly as widespread as the one at Passover.

In Israel today the celebration of Tu B'Shevat is linked with replanting forests that existed long ago. Classes of schoolchildren plant trees (see below). In the diaspora Jews may raise money to pay for these new trees, and to help poorer families buy fruit for the Tu B'Shevat seder.

In recent years, Jewish environmentalists have revived Tu B'Shevat as an 'eco-festival'. They see it as the ideal moment to celebrate traditional Jewish connections to nature, to learn and teach about trees and to take environmental action.

ACTIVITY

Either:
In groups, imagine you are planning an afternoon of activities for members of a synagogue to celebrate Tu B'Shevat. Try and include a range of activities that will appeal to all ages.
Or:
Design a dedication plaque for a tree planted at Tu B'Shevat. You might include decoration and a relevant Jewish quotation.

SAVE AS...

Tu B'Shevat has several meanings for Jews today. Copy this table and explain how each meaning can be observed. Use Sources A and B and page 76.

Meaning	How this is observed
Caring for trees	
Celebrating God's renewal of nature	
Raising awareness of our connections to nature	

A

We always make a special effort to beautify the table with flowers and leaves. As part of the Tu B'Shevat seder we try and eat at least fifteen varieties of fruit, to represent the '15' that is the date of the festival. We eat them in three separate rounds. First those that have a hard outside, like oranges and walnuts. Then those with a hard inside, like dates and olives. Lastly, those such as figs or strawberries that are edible throughout.

We also need to set out red and white wine or grape juice. During the seder we drink four cups of wine, from winter-white to the deep red of autumn. Sometimes we also have on the table the seven species with which Israel has been blessed – wheat, barley, grapes, figs, pomegranates, olives and dates. We may start the seder by eating these in the order in which they appear in Deuteronomy 8.8.

Apart from blessing God for creating the fruit and wine, and then eating and drinking, the form of the seder is up to us. We have put together our own seder haggadah, which includes our favourite Jewish texts, poems and songs about trees and nature. Everyone takes a turn to read. At the end of the evening we try to plant a tree in the garden, so that we will have put our words into action.

A Tu B'Shevat seder

B

a) On Tu B'Shevat
When spring comes,
An angel descends, ledger in hand,
And enters each bud, each twig, each tree,
And all our garden flowers.
From town to town, from village to village,
The angel makes a winged way,
Searching the valleys, inspecting the hills,
Flying over the desert
And returns to heaven.
And when the ledger will be full
Of trees and blossoms and shrubs,
When the desert is turned into a meadow
And all our land is a watered garden,
The Messiah will appear.

Shin Shalom

b) While the sage Honi was walking along a road, he saw a man planting a carob tree.
Honi asked him, 'How long will it take for this tree to bear fruit?'
'Seventy years,' replied the man.
Honi then asked, 'Are you so healthy a man that you expect to live that length of time and eat its fruit?'
The man answered, 'I found a fruitful world because my ancestors planted it for me. Likewise I am planting for my children.'

Babylonian Talmud

c) It is forbidden to live in a town that does not have greenery.

Jerusalem Talmud

Extracts from a Tu B'Shevat haggadah

Humans have an important role

There is no doubt in Judaism that what humans do matters. If humans follow God's commandments, nature will work as it was intended to do. If they do not, it will not.

C

Upon creating the first human beings, God guided them around the Garden of Eden, saying: 'Look at my creations! See how beautiful and perfect they are! For your sake I created them all. Make sure you don't ruin or devastate my world. If you do, there will be no one else to repair it.'

Ecclesiastes Rabbah 7.13

D

Take care not to be lured away to serve other gods . . . For the Lord's anger will flare up against you; and He will shut up the skies so that there will be no rain and the ground will not yield its produce; and you will soon perish from the good land that the Lord is assigning to you.

Deuteronomy 11.16–17

E

"Hello! We can't be far from civilisation"

Responsibility

Although God is the Creator of the world, people are the caretakers, or stewards, of creation. Adam and Eve's role in the Garden of Eden was 'to till it and tend it' (Genesis 2.15), and this is how people should act in the world. The Earth belongs to God (Psalm 24) – humans have the use of it only for their lifetimes. Since people are made in the image of God, they are obliged to take care of other species in the same way that God does.

Jews see one of their jobs as continuing the work of creation by constantly making the world a better and holier place. One way of repairing the world (in Hebrew, 'tikkun olam') is to heal the environment. Jewish tradition has many guidelines for doing this:

- Do not waste or destroy (in Hebrew 'bal tashchit'). Any needless waste of food, possessions or other resources is wrong.
- Do not cause distress to living creatures (in Hebrew, 'tsa'ar ba'alei chayim'). Jews must look after animals with compassion.
- Prevent pollution. There are guidelines in the Torah and the Talmud about waste disposal, green belts, noise, and pollution of air and water.
- The land and the people are closely connected. Just as people must take time off from work each Shabbat, the land too is entitled to a year's break from being planted every seventh year. At the end of seven cycles of seven years, in the 50th year, all land is to be returned to its original owner.

Wonder and amazement

It's not all hard work, though. The natural world is also a source of inspiration and wonder. Throughout the sacred texts of Judaism nature itself is described as praising God (see Psalms 96, 98 and 148 for examples). When Jews are struck by the wonders of nature, there are special blessings they can say (see Source F).

F

Blessed are you, Lord our God, King of the Universe . . .

. . . who makes the work of creation.

. . . for nothing is lacking in His universe, and He created in it good creatures and good trees, to cause mankind pleasure with them.

. . . who made the great sea.

ACTIVITY

1. From the sources on this page write three 'rules for eco-living', i.e. rules to guide Jews in how to care for their environment.
2. Use your rules to make a poster, or a series of three posters (one for each rule). Your poster should express the rules clearly and simply, but also describe in words or show in pictures an example of how it might be applied (or what will go wrong if it is not applied).
3. Send your completed posters to The Noah Project (your teacher can give you the address).

SAVE AS...

4. Copy this diagram.

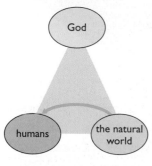

5. Add arrows and labels to show the relationships that are described or hinted at on this page. For example; the natural world gives humans a glimpse of God.

The Noah Project

Vivienne Cato (one of the authors of this book) is a Jew who has always been interested in the environment and the natural world. She now works in Jewish education and runs sessions for teachers on Judaism and the environment. She is a founder member of The Noah Project, an educational and campaigning group that has been set up by Jewish environmentalists across Britain. Their leaflet explains its aims and objectives (Source H).

G

My starting point

A few years ago I spent some time in the United States, and I discovered two things. First, that Judaism had a lot to say about the environment, and second, that a lot of Jews there were making that connection public! When I came back I wanted to create some interest in this topic here in Britain. Gradually I found some like-minded people and together we decided to set up the first national Jewish environmental group in this country. After a lot of discussion about names, we chose The Noah Project.

Aims

We are all committed to both Judaism and environmentalism, but we want to reach two other main groups of people. One is observant Jews who aren't so aware of how 'green' Judaism is. The other is secular Jews who are already environmentalists but who haven't realised that Judaism relates to their concerns.

The environment unites Jews

We have already collected a long list of names of interested people and have got support from rabbis across the religious spectrum. In Judaism the environment is a less contentious issue than, say, women's rights. No rabbi is going to find our standpoint objectionable in Jewish law! So, in principle, everyone can rally behind us. In practice, though, there are conflicting priorities. For example, Orthodox Jews may provide only disposable plates and cutlery at a celebration to make sure they are absolutely kosher. Yet throwing away all this non-biodegradable material after only one use contravenes the law of Bal Tashchit – do not waste. But this is a lot less important than what unites us.

The future

We are now planning our work for the next few years. Our logo says 'Jewish Education, Celebration and Action for the Earth'. So we are trying to plan projects that fall into each of these categories. At the moment we are aiming to write a curriculum in Jewish Environmental Education for use in primary schools. We also want to get synagogues and Jewish homes doing more recycling and energy-saving. We hope that in five years we will be an established fixture on the British Jewish landscape.

Vivienne Cato

H

JUDAISM AND THE ENVIRONMENT

Have you ever wondered how a text over a thousand years old could tell us anything about the care of the environment today?

Teachings throughout the Torah demonstrate how we should relate to our environment; there are teachings on the needless waste of resources, animal welfare, food ethics, rest for the land and biodiversity.

The rabbis expanded on these teachings in the Talmud in their discussions on air pollution, urban green belts, hazardous waste, water quality, and more.

Or perhaps you already know how 'green' issues permeate Jewish teaching, but haven't found others who share your interest?

We are a group of environmentally committed Jews seeking other like-minded people to join us in THE NOAH PROJECT. We believe that green issues touch all of us and we wish to join with Jews across the spectrum of Judaism and with those who are unaffiliated.

Or maybe you and your friends have talked about these ideas but you haven't found a forum for practical action?

THE NOAH PROJECT exists to promote environmental activity within the Jewish community through education, celebration and action.

THE OBJECTIVES OF THE NOAH PROJECT

- Build a national network through synagogues and other Jewish organisations to promote green awareness.
- Promote and produce environmental materials for education for adults and children.
- Add a Jewish voice to the secular and interfaith environmental movements.
- Encourage recognition of the links between the rhythms of the Earth and the rhythms of the Jewish Shabbat and festival cycles.
- Stimulate and co-ordinate practical action to promote stewardship of the environment.

A leaflet explaining the aims and objectives of The Noah Project

I

Noah Project members on a Jewish nature walk for Sukkot

DISCUSS

Rabbi Tarfon (1st century CE) said, 'It is not for you to finish the task, but neither are you free to desist from it.'

1 Discuss what Rabbi Tarfon means.
2 Discuss how you think The Noah Project helps Jews follow Rabbi Tarfon's teaching.

What rights do animals have?

Jewish law forbids cruelty to living things – Tsa'ar ba'alei chayim (see page 79). This goes as far back as the story of Noah who, after the flood, was told not to get meat by tearing the limbs from living animals. The animal must be killed first. The system of ritual Jewish slaughter (SHECHITA) that developed subsequently is intended to kill an animal as quickly and painlessly as possible. No animal must witness its parent or child being killed.

Although cruelty is not permitted, a range of views on animals can be found within Judaism.

	On the one hand . . .	On the other hand . . .
Are animal rights equal to human rights?	In the Creation story, humans were made last. This implies that they are the most important of God's creations. Adam was given the responsibility of naming the animals (Genesis 2.19) and ruling over them (Genesis 1.28). This suggests that people's role is one of stewardship. Animals do not have rights equal to humans.	The fourth of the Ten Commandments requires working animals to have a day of rest, just like their owners. Jews are obliged to attend to an animal's need for food before their own, and to take care even of stray animals.
Should Jews be vegetarian?	In the Garden of Eden, which is thought of as paradise, humans were not allowed to eat meat or fish, only fruits and vegetables. God first allowed people to eat meat after the Flood, when humans had been almost wiped out for behaving wickedly. For some Jews, vegetarianism is the ideal; Isaiah's vision of the future is: 'In all of My sacred mount nothing evil or vile shall be done' (Isaiah 11.9). To sanctify food and respect its Creator, a blessing must be said before eating anything. There are special blessings for fruit and vegetables, but no blessing specifically for meat.	The system of kashrut (KOSHER food) allows meat to be eaten, but only within limits. Its main requirements are that: • only meat from animals that chew the cud and have cloven hooves, and fish that have both fins and scales may be eaten • meat and milk products may not be consumed at the same meal • meat animals must be killed in a prescribed way (shechita), which was devised to cause the animal the least possible pain. Some Jews argue that factory-farmed animals can never be kosher because they are kept in conditions of cruelty.
What about blood sports?	Jews are not allowed to hunt, or to trap animals for their fur. Only animals slaughtered specifically and in the prescribed manner for food are kosher, so animals killed for sport could not be eaten.	Hunting for food is permitted if the animal is trapped, no pain is caused, and then it is killed in the prescribed way.

ACTIVITY

1 Jews are allowed to own animals and use them for work – but only within certain conditions. Make a list of these conditions.

2 According to Jewish thinking, which, if any, would you find in the kosher butcher in Source J:
   a) battery eggs
   b) chickens
   c) cheeseburgers (a beefburger with cheese)?
   Give reasons for your answers and explain why there might be different Jewish points of view.

SAVE AS...

3 Design a sign for the shop window in Source J explaining to the public what a kosher butcher is and what they can and cannot buy there.

J

A kosher butcher in Paris

SAVE AS...

Copy this table into your book. Find the quotations in your Bible and read them carefully. Summarise the quotations in the first column and tick the columns to which each quotation applies.

	Considers humans first	Considers animals first
'Do not buy an animal before buying food for that animal to eat.' Jerusalem Talmud, Ketubot 4.8		
Genesis 9.3		
Deuteronomy 25.4		
Deuteronomy 5.14		
Exodus 23.5		
'A righteous man knows the needs of his beast . . .' Proverbs 12.10		

FOCUS TASK

'God said, "...Fill the earth and master it; and rule the fish of the sea, the birds of the sky, and all the living things that creep on earth."' (Genesis 1.28)

In class, hold a debate on whether Judaism allows humans to exploit nature. Use the information on pages 76–83 to help you.

4.3   Can Jews fight for peace?

A

1   Look at Source A.
Could these events
happen by the year
2020? Explain your
view.

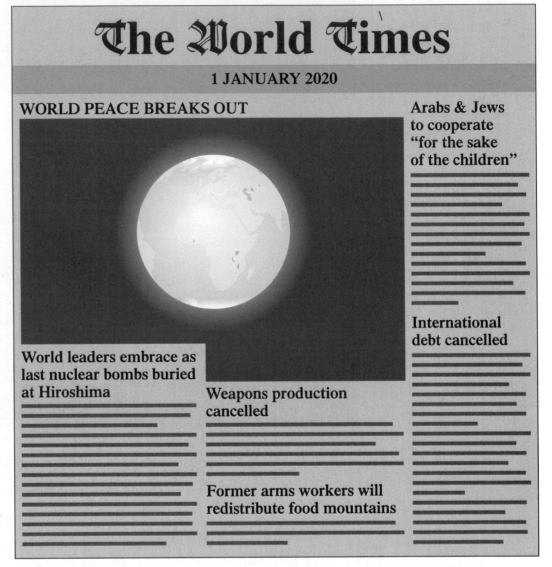

The World Times

1 JANUARY 2020

WORLD PEACE BREAKS OUT

Arabs & Jews to cooperate "for the sake of the children"

International debt cancelled

World leaders embrace as last nuclear bombs buried at Hiroshima

Weapons production cancelled

Former arms workers will redistribute food mountains

B

a) *Establish peace, goodness, blessing, graciousness, kindness and compassion upon us and upon all of your people Israel ... And may it be good in your eyes to bless your people Israel in every season and every hour with your peace. Blessed are you God who blesses his people Israel with peace.*

From the AMIDAH prayer

b) *He who makes peace in his heights, may he make peace upon us, and upon all Israel.*

From the Amidah prayer

c) *The Lord will give strength to his people; the Lord will bless his people with peace.*

Psalm 29.11, part of grace after meals (from the *Good News Bible*)

Look back at the history of Judaism on pages 6–9. It might strike you as fairly violent. Yet despite this (or maybe because of it) Judaism values peace above all else.

Jewish prayers (see examples in Source B) look forward to a state of peace. The Torah, the Talmud and Jewish writers all instruct Jews to pursue peace (see Source C). Each week Shabbat is intended to bring an interval of peace to people's troubled everyday lives (see page 4).

The big idea is SHALOM. Shalom means peace or wholeness. It is also the Hebrew word for 'hallo' and 'goodbye'. To a Jewish believer, shalom is much more than absence of war. It is also the perfect state of the world after the Messiah comes (see Source D) and it is something that Jews hope for and work for in the present.

You can see that shalom is a big idea and an ever-present idea. Shalom = peace = wholeness = perfection.

C

a) *He who makes peace in his house, it is as if he made peace in all of Israel. But he who brings jealousy and strife into his house, it is as if he brought them among all Israel.*

Gamaliel II who lived in Palestine at the end of the first century CE

b) *In God's eyes the man stands high who makes peace between men – between husband and wife, between parents and children, between management and labour, between neighbour and neighbour. But he stands highest who establishes peace among the nations.*

Talmud

c) *Work for peace within your household, then in your street, then in your town.*

The Bershider Rabbi (died 1816)

D

a) *They shall beat their swords into ploughshares, and their spears into pruning hooks: nation shall not take up sword against nation; they shall never again know war.*

Isaiah 2.4

b) *The wolf shall dwell with the lamb,
The leopard lie down with the kid;
The calf, the beast of prey and the fatling together,
With a little boy to herd them.
The cow and the bear shall graze,
Their young shall lie down together;
And the lion, like the ox, shall eat straw...
In all of my sacred mount
Nothing evil or vile shall be done;
For the land shall be filled with devotion to the Lord
As water covers the sea.*

Isaiah 11.6–9

E

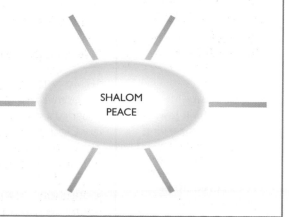

A prize-winning entry in 'Bible 2000', an international art competition for schoolchildren. The text along the top of the scroll is the names of the first five books of the Torah, and the word at the bottom says 'shalom'.

DISCUSS

1 **What do the writers in Source C agree about?**
2 **What do they disagree about?**
3 **Which source do you most agree with?**
4 **How could you help create peace:**
   a) in your 'household'
   b) in your 'street'
   c) in your school?

SAVE AS...

5 **Complete this spider diagram to record the Jewish ideas about peace outlined in the sources and text on these two pages.**
6 **Write a paragraph recording your reactions to the Jewish ideas about peace in your spider diagram.**

SHALOM
PEACE

1   Read Source F. Why do you think the Bible forbids cutting down fruit trees in war?

F

When in your war against a city you have to besiege it a long time in order to capture it, you must not destroy its [fruit] trees, wielding the axe against them. You may eat of them, but you must not cut them down. Are trees of the field human to withdraw before you into the besieged city? Only trees that you know do not yield fruit may be destroyed; you may cut them down for constructing siegeworks against the city that is waging war on you, until it has been [captured].

Deuteronomy 20.19–20

ACTIVITY

1   Complete this sentence as many times as you wish: 'I would fight in a war if . . .'

2   Compare your sentences with a partner's, then discuss:
a) which of your reasons, if any, follow Jewish teaching?
b) which of your reasons, if any, are against Jewish teaching?

SAVE AS . . .

3   Do you think Jewish principles regarding war are useful today? Explain your view showing that you have considered other points of view.

Just war

The ideas on the previous page were quite idealistic. Yet Judaism is a very realistic religion. So what do Jews do about real conflict in the real world?
There is no single Jewish view but there are some agreed principles:

- **War is always regrettable,** even when it is necessary. The Bible says that the reason King David – the great hero of Israel – was not allowed by God to build the temple was because he was 'a man of battles and [had] shed blood.'
- **War can be justified only in self-defence.** There are examples of wars in Jewish history that were not self-defence, but these are not models for today.

Individual self-defence

Within Judaism you can find rules for how an individual should defend themselves when attacked. The Talmud instructs, 'If a person intends to kill you, be first to kill him.' (Sanhedrin 72a). However, a key commandment of Judaism is to preserve life at all costs, so the teaching adds that if maiming someone is enough to deflect the attacker then killing them would be murder, not self-defence.

Milchemet mitzvah = obligatory war

These principles of individual self-defence have been extended into the case of wars between nations. In Judaism, a war is a just war if:

- the enemy has attacked you first
- you need to pre-empt an attack (this can be difficult to define).

These are cases for MILCHEMET MITZVAH – war that you have to undertake. However, there are conditions for the way such a war must be fought:

- war must be a last resort
- non-violent approaches to the dispute must have been tried first
- civilians must not be targeted
- damage must be minimised (see Source F).

Milchemet reshut = optional war

All other war would be MILCHEMET RESHUT – one that has been entered into of one's own accord. It is supposed to be entered into only after consultation with the religious authorities. These authorities have not permitted such a war since the time of the Temple, nearly 2000 years ago.

War for any of the following reasons is not allowed in Jewish teaching:

- to create political advantage
- to enhance national security where it has not been threatened
- if it destroys entirely whatever is growing (a 'scorched earth' policy)
- if it targets civilians specifically, as opposed to incidentally
- if its sole purpose is to inspire militarism.

Is there such a thing as 'holy war'?

'Holy war' is not a term used by Jews today, nor is there such a phrase in modern Hebrew, because in Judaism the concept does not exist. Although some battles described in the Bible were started aggressively and were apparently approved by God, nothing like this has taken place in the 2000 years that have passed since those events. The idea of waging war to promote certain beliefs or to conquer other peoples or lands is not possible in modern Jewish teaching.
Milchemet mitzvah, Judaism's concept of a just war, takes place under conditions commanded by God. But there is nothing holy about it. It is merely a war one is obliged to fight in self-defence.

G

For I cannot help withstanding evil when I see that it is about to destroy the good. I am forced to withstand the evil in the world just as the evil within myself. I can only strive not to have to do so by force. I do not want force. But if there is no other way of preventing the evil destroying the good, I trust I shall use force and give myself up into God's hands.

Martin Buber, a Jewish philosopher, writing to Gandhi, the leader of the movement for Indian independence. Gandhi, a Hindu opposed to all forms of violence, led a campaign of passive resistance.

DISCUSS

The data cards on the right outline two conflicts in the twentieth century that involved hard decisions for Jewish people. They only give you the bare details of each conflict.

How far do you think action in these conflicts was consistent with the Jewish teaching on war outlined on these two pages?

Are there Jewish pacifists?

True pacifism, which opposes fighting wars in any circumstances, is a marginal view in Judaism. Most Jews believe in the right to self-defence when one's safety is threatened.

Some ultra-Orthodox groups in Israel are exempt from army service, being allowed instead to pursue their religious studies, but this is not for reasons of pacifism. They feel that Torah study is a higher religious obligation than warfare, and that it is the best way to protect the Jewish people.

Others among the ultra-Orthodox refuse to serve because they do not recognise the secular authority of the Israeli government. They believe that Jewish rule in the land of Israel is not legitimate until the arrival of the MESSIAH (see page 116). Source G is a more typical Jewish reaction to pacifism.

Case study 1: the Warsaw Ghetto uprising, 1943

The Nazis captured Warsaw in 1939. They ordered all 400,000 of its Jews into a ghetto, a confined and walled area of the town of less than three square kilometres. Four years later, the Nazis began mass deportations from the ghetto to the concentration camp of Treblinka. By spring 1943, the Jewish underground learned of plans for the destruction of the remaining 50,000 Jews. Led by the 1000 members of the ghetto's fighting organisation, and armed only with a few guns and some home-made bombs, these Jews took the invading Nazi forces by surprise. It took the Germans four weeks of heavy fighting to raze the ghetto to the ground, after which they gassed those still hidden in underground bunkers. Only a few Jews escaped alive from this battle.

Case study 2: the Six-Day War, 1967

The State of Israel was founded in 1948. The land given to Israel had been home to Jews and Palestinian Arabs and was being ruled by Britain. From the start, Israel faced constant conflict with neighbouring Arab countries, particularly Syria, Egypt and Jordan. Syria joined Egypt and Jordan in a military alliance against Israel. Proclaiming that Israel would be driven into the sea, President Nasser of Egypt forced the United Nations troops to withdraw from their buffer position in the Sinai desert. Taking this as an act of war, on 5 June Israel sent

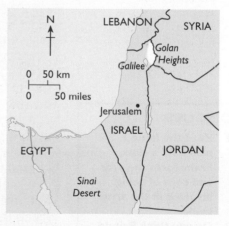

its planes on a pre-emptive strike against Egyptian, Jordanian and Syrian air-bases, and destroyed 450 enemy planes on the ground. Israel offered peace, but King Hussein of Jordan ordered an attack on Jerusalem. Consequently, Israel attacked Jordan and gained control of the Jordanian-occupied West Bank and the Old City of Jerusalem, which had not been under Jewish control for 2000 years. The Syrians, fighting from the Golan Heights, were similarly defeated by the Israeli Air Force. The war was over in only six days.

The State of Israel – balancing contradictions

Although a large part of Israel's population is Jewish, Israel is not a 'Jewish' state; it is a secular state run by elected politicians, not by rabbis. However, most of Israel's citizens and its leaders are Jews who take the teachings and practices of Judaism very seriously. The government is under pressure to follow Jewish teaching in its political decisions and a strong minority of religious Jews inside and outside politics try to influence them to do so. They would say that in the Bible the Jews were commanded to be 'a kingdom of priests and a holy nation' (Exodus 19.6) – that is, to conduct politics and warfare according to spiritual values.

As you'd expect, this is not easy. In the real world moral issues seldom have easy solutions!

You have already studied one example of Israel in action in the Six-Day War. Israel's defenders would argue that Israel acted solely in self-defence (and therefore within the definition of milchemet mitzvah). Its critics argue that Israel went beyond what was needed for self-defence and that it was a war of aggression (and therefore against religious principles) that harmed civilians and also created problems for the future. The debate continues, as does the tension between Israel and its Arab neighbours. You will return to this on pages 90–91.

What is very clear is that Israel has come to depend on its strong armed forces for its security. This has raised some dilemmas for ordinary Jews living in Israel. You are going to examine two of the issues and discuss parallels in your own country today.

1 Look back at Source D on page 85. What point is the cartoon in Source H making?
2 How would you reply to this cartoon if you were:
   a) a religious Jew who was concerned about Israel's arms trade
   b) a secular Jew who supported Israel's right to sell arms?

H

They shall beat their swords into ploughshares... (*Isaiah Ch.2,V.4*)

This cartoon appeared in *The Times* in 1996.

Issue 1: the arms trade

In its early years Israel did not make its own weapons. It bought them from other countries, particularly France. In the Six-Day War, France supported the Arab alliance. Afterwards it refused to sell weapons to Israel. Israel began manufacturing its own arms, such as fighter planes and ship-to-ship missiles. It went on to become a supplier of such weapons to other countries, too.

All countries that sell arms are presented with ethical problems, and Israel is no exception. Should weapons be sold at all? Selling to one's enemies may be avoided, but what about to one's allies? Should allies be supplied with arms even if they pursue some policies that may not be ethical?

Israeli export of arms is in principle governed by Jewish law, which does not permit the sale of arms to powers which will abuse them, for example, using them to harm their own people, or to attack another country. Under Jewish law, weapons can only be sold to be used in self-defence.

However, the Israeli state-owned defence industry, one of the world's leading exporters in this field, has sold weapons to countries that have been accused of violating human rights.

The only sure way for a country to prevent its weapons being used unethically by another country is for it to stop making or selling them. But the arms trade is a lucrative business and Israel needs weapons for its own self-defence. How do you resolve this dilemma?

DISCUSS

1 Read the Issue 1 panel. As a class, brainstorm the pros and cons of being involved in the arms trade.
2 Do you think Britain should be involved in the arms trade?
   a) If not, explain your reasons.
   b) If yes, suggest three simple ethical rules to guide the sale of arms.

Issue 2: military service

As with its government, the Israeli military is a secular institution, even though many of its individual soldiers hold strong religious principles. Some ultra-Orthodox Jews are exempt from service (see page 87). However, with the exception of these groups, or those who cannot take part for medical reasons, all Israelis must give time to the Israel Defense Forces (IDF – the army and other armed forces). This is in contrast to Britain, which ended compulsory national service in 1962.

From the age of fourteen, both boys and girls in Israel receive military training in the youth corps. At the age of eighteen, when in Britain many young people are starting university or work, all eligible Israelis begin military service, boys for three years and girls for two. They therefore can only start their higher education after this. Not all serve in fighting units; some work in administration or catering. For the next 30 years of their lives, men are called up each year for 30 days of reserve duty, which can be doubled in times of emergency.

Some argue that this keeps Israel strong and able to defend itself. It is widely accepted that military service is a normal and worthwhile part of each person's life. During the Six-Day War (see page 87) volunteers from around the world flocked to help Israel defend itself.

I

In Israel, armed teenage soldiers are a common sight.

DISCUSS

1 **Do you think Britain should reintroduce compulsory national service? Give reasons.**
2 **Should anyone be exempt from serving?**

J

When the Six-Day War broke out, I had just got married. Like Jews everywhere, we felt there was a real danger that Israel could be destroyed. We, like so many others, announced to our families and employers that we were volunteering to go and help in any way needed.

Airports were crowded with Jewish people of all ages waiting for flights to Israel. Before we knew it, the war was over and by the time most of the volunteers arrived in Israel it was a question of filling in, mainly in the kibbutzim (collective farms), for those who had been on the front lines, and who were going to be on duty for some time to come. We spent three great months picking fruit, as the kibbutz we were sent to had 106 people in the army. Four were tragically killed in the battle for the Old City of Jerusalem.

Naomi Cohen

However, a small minority of Jews regard military service as a problem.

K

I grew up absorbing the Jewish notion of the value of life. And since Jews were never previously part of the power structure in society, there was an instinctive taboo against using weapons. All this inclined me towards pacifism [although I did my military service]. The miracle of my first child's birth forced me to question whether I could take any life. I began to find it difficult to serve in the army. I declined to take part in military manoeuvres, and went on hunger strike. I refused even to carry a gun. Eventually the army declined to draft me for reserve duty.

With the creation of their own country in the State of Israel, Jews became like everyone else. But this led to the use of force, and to racism, which is maintained through violence. The only honourable thing to do was to serve in the army – you had to be extremely strong to resist. Non-violence is not much spoken about in public, so Israelis don't know they have the option to serve or not. We rely on others to be violent on our behalf. But it's important that people recognise that there is an alternative way to live, through pursuing dialogue and hospitality with your neighbour. We need to promote non-violence and partnership through justice.

Jeremy Milgrom is a rabbi who lives and works in Jerusalem. He is active in reconciling Jews and Palestinians.

It's a classic dilemma: the needs of the government versus the scruples of an individual. How do you resolve this contradiction?

Yitzhak Rabin (1922–95): soldier for peace

A soldier turned diplomat, Yitzhak Rabin was a native Israeli, born in Jerusalem. Originally trained in agriculture, he joined the underground liberation fighters who aimed to free Palestine, as it then was, from British rule. One consequence of this was a six-month spell in prison under British arrest. During the War of Independence in 1948 he commanded a brigade and was actively involved in the battle for Jerusalem. As Chief of Staff of the IDF, he led the country to victory in the Six-Day War. His move into politics came with his appointment as Israel's ambassador to the United States. He subsequently became Prime Minister (1974–77) and was re-elected almost two decades later, in 1992.

Nobel peace prize

On 13 September 1993, following many months of first secret and then open negotiations, Rabin as Prime Minister of Israel and Yasir Arafat, Chairman of the Palestine Liberation Organisation (PLO), signed a peace agreement in Washington under the supervision of President Clinton. In so doing, each recognised the other's right to exist, which they had always previously refused to do. For this, they were jointly presented with the Nobel Prize for Peace.

Were Israelis ready for peace?

The State of Israel had not been free from war, actual and threatened, since its establishment in 1948. Every family had suffered bereavements and casualties, or knew others who had. They also looked forward to the 'peace dividend': the boost that peace would bring to the economy. Rabin was probably one of the few leaders who was acceptable to Israelis as a peacemaker, since he had already proved himself as a military hero.

However, Israel's citizens were split regarding the peace agreement. Many, while wanting peace, did not trust Arafat and the PLO, and were suspicious of what the future would bring.

On 4 November 1995, at a peace rally in Tel Aviv, Rabin was shot by 25-year-old Yigal Amir, a Jewish law student and ex-combat soldier. He shot as Rabin left the stage, having just led a crowd of 100,000 in singing the Song of Peace. The spot soon became a shrine to the dead Prime Minister, as shocked Israelis congregated there to mourn, place flowers and light memorial candles.

The next election after Rabin's death was narrowly won by the Likud Party who opposed making concessions to Israel's enemies in the search for peace.

DISCUSS

1. Read Source L. How does Yigal Amir justify his assassination of Rabin?
2. What do you think about Amir's action? Give reasons for your answer.

SAVE AS...

3. Write two messages to be posted at Rabin's memorial. One should be by an admirer, the other by a critic.

L

Judge: *In the Ten Commandments it says, 'Thou shalt not kill.' Where have you thrown the Ten Commandments?*

Amir: *The Ten Commandments haven't been abolished. In the Torah there are 613 commandments. There are commandments more important than 'Thou shalt not kill.' There's 'the saving of life'. If someone goes to kill another person, you are duty-bound to kill the attacker first.*

From Yigal Amir's trial in *Yitzhak Rabin: Soldier of Peace*. Amir believed that, in making concessions to the Palestinians, Rabin had endangered Jewish lives.

M

Israelis mourning Rabin in the days immediately following his death. The Yarzheit candles (see page 27) are a sign of respect.

Neve Shalom: building a community for peace

Jews believe that the Messiah is yet to come, and that with his arrival will come a state of 'shalom', of peace. Jews believe they have a role to play here: they are required to work to make the world a more perfect and peaceful place in order to hasten the Messiah's arrival. Some Reform Jews do not believe in the concept of an individual Messiah but rather in a Messianic age.

The village of Neve Shalom/Wahat al-Salam (its name means 'Oasis of Peace' in Hebrew and Arabic) was founded in 1972 by a Dominican monk, Father Bruno Hussar. His vision was of a community in which all peoples lived together in peace. He believed that ten per cent of a population co-operating is enough to change the direction of a democratic society towards peace. Today Neve Shalom is still the only co-operative village in Israel, democratically owned and governed by Jewish and Arab citizens who have chosen to live alongside each other. Believing that children learn to live in peace 'in the cradle', the villagers have established a 'School for Peace'. Children from both groups learn together in Hebrew and Arabic, from Jewish and Arab teachers, and from each other. The school's success and growth mean that three-quarters of its pupils now come from outside the village, from the surrounding region.

Neve Shalom also hosts programmes for young people, for teachers and for other professionals working for Palestinian–Jewish reconciliation, to promote understanding between Arabs and Jews.

N

If I want to be listened to, it's important I learn to listen.

We sat and talked, and suddenly she cried, 'I understand you!' It was a breakthrough.

I feel that I'm taking the people here with me. I hope we don't have to meet on the battlefield.

These are real views expressed by young people who have taken part in programmes at Neve Shalom's School for Peace. You can find more examples on its website (see Focus Task).

Tom Kita'in was a graduate of Neve Shalom's School for Peace who was killed in 1997 in a helicopter accident whilst on army service. Another 72 young soldiers died with him. Interviewed by his community's newsletter six months in to his army service he had said, 'I must serve my country, but I detest war. I do not want to shoot . . . I feel that my life will be affected very strongly if I know that I have killed someone . . . All this creates in me a dilemma.'

At Tom's memorial service at his high school, his mother, Daniella Kita'in, said, 'Sometimes, maybe always, added to the great pain is a sour feeling of missed opportunity. For me this sour feeling is connected to the fact that I, who always believed in the way of peace, could not save my eldest son from an accident of war.'

Global issues - Review tasks

A

1 Explain the meaning of the term 'tzedakah'.
2 How is the organisation shown in this photograph giving tzedakah?
3 State and explain one quotation from the Torah which would encourage a Jew to give tzedakah.
4 Describe the work of one Jewish organisation involved in helping to relieve poverty.
5 'Jewish agencies should look after the poor of their own religion before they look after those of other religions.' Do you agree? Explain your answer, showing that you have considered other points of view.

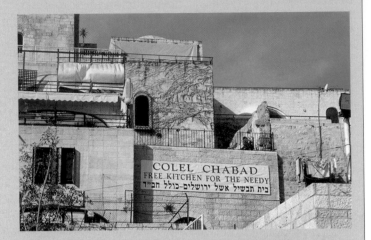

B

1 What is Tu B'Shevat?
2 Outline two ways in which Tu B'Shevat encourages Jews to look after the environment.
3 'If humans live as God intends then nature will work as God intends.' Do you agree? Give reasons for your answer, showing that you have thought about other points of view. You must refer to Judaism in your answer.

C

1 Explain the meaning of the term 'shalom'.
2 Describe two situations in which Jewish teaching would oblige Jews to go to war.
3 Explain how Jews would apply the commandment 'You shall not murder' in the context of war.
4 'You cannot be a Jew and a pacifist.' Explain whether you agree or disagree with this statement, showing that you have considered other points of view.

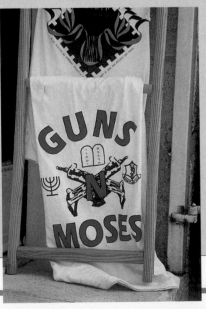

UNIT 5

Thinking about God

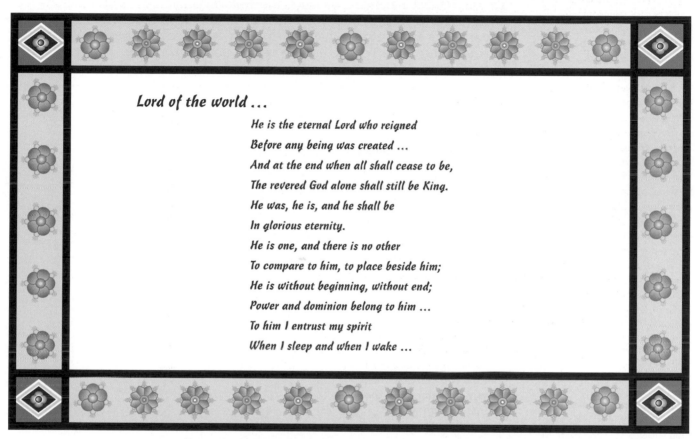

Lord of the world ...

> *He is the eternal Lord who reigned*
> *Before any being was created ...*
> *And at the end when all shall cease to be,*
> *The revered God alone shall still be King.*
> *He was, he is, and he shall be*
> *In glorious eternity.*
> *He is one, and there is no other*
> *To compare to him, to place beside him;*
> *He is without beginning, without end;*
> *Power and dominion belong to him ...*
> *To him I entrust my spirit*
> *When I sleep and when I wake ...*

From the 'Adon Olam', which is sung at the end of Shabbat and festival services and has many different tunes. It expresses the constant presence and oneness of God in the world.

In this unit you will investigate Jewish beliefs in greater depth. Some ideas might be new to you. Others might feel familiar. Some beliefs might be ones you share. Others you might disagree with. Whatever your own beliefs, this unit aims to help you understand what Jews believe about God, to compare those beliefs with your own and to help you express your own views clearly and convincingly.

Arguing and discussion are a natural part of everyday life. They are also the best way to clarify ideas. Someone has an idea. Someone else disagrees with it. They argue. One persuades the other, or not, depending on whether their arguments are convincing. This is how philosophers work. It is also how Jewish teachers often work. In Judaism there is a long tradition of debate and argument about what God is like and how God may be known.

So to get you in the right frame of mind, write five statements about God that you personally agree with. You can do this even if you do not believe that God exists. Then as a class see if you can come up with a single statement from all the statements class members have written – just one – that *all the class can agree with*. Just one statement. Your teacher can give you some statements to get you started.

5.1   What is God like?

For your exam you will need to use the following words and apply them to Jewish beliefs.

MONOTHEISM means believing in one God.

POLYTHEISM means believing in more than one god.

IMMANENT means 'in the world or universe'. An immanent God is able and willing to act in human affairs.

TRANSCENDENT means 'outside or beyond the natural world or universe'. A transcendent God is not limited by space or time, and does not act in human affairs.

PERSONAL: a personal God is close to human beings in their day-to-day lives.

The opposite idea is that God is IMPERSONAL: more like a source of light, or an abstract force or energy than like a person.

The terms immanent and transcendent, personal and impersonal are opposites. It is likely that for every person who holds one view there will be one who holds the opposite. God is like that! Then there will be others who will say that both ideas are true at the same time, even if they are conflicting ideas. God is by nature beyond human abilities so may be beyond human understanding. Religious writing is often an attempt to describe the indescribable. So opposites and contradictions are sometimes quite helpful.

God or G-d?
Some Jews write the word God as G-d in case the paper is accidentally damaged, or treated without respect. Others do not speak or write the name of God except in prayers, because God is too holy.

One of the best ways of finding out how religious believers view God is to look at their prayers, particularly prayers that are addressed to God.

Orthodox and Reform Jews use the same central prayers, such as Sources B and C, although the Orthodox use Hebrew versions, while the Reform sometimes use translations into their own language. Reform prayerbooks also include extra readings, taken from different sources and adapted to modern belief. Orthodox prayerbooks include ideas that Reform Jews do not accept, such as praying for the rebuilding of the Temple and the restoration of sacrifices.

ACTIVITY

You are going to see what Jewish prayers tell you about Jewish beliefs about God.

Work in groups. Read Sources A–G and the 'Adon Olam' on page 93 and find words and phrases used to describe God or ideas about God. A few have been highlighted to get you started. (See Sources C, D and E.)

Use your words to complete a diagram like the one opposite.

Read the Checkpoint before you start to make sure you understand the words immanent and transcendent.

A

My God, the soul you have placed in me is pure; you it was who created it, you formed it, you blew it into me, you guard it within me, you will take it from me, and return it to me, in time-to-be.

Talmud, Berachot 60b – used in the morning service

B

Blessed are you, O Lord our God, King of the universe who forms light and creates darkness, who makes peace and creates all things.

From the morning service

C

Blessed are thou, O Lord our God who ... gives food to all flesh, for your mercy endures forever ... Blessed are you who feeds all living things.

From grace after meals

D

You O Lord, are the endless power that renews life beyond death; You are the greatness that saves You care for the living with love. You renew life beyond death with unending mercy You support the falling and heal the sick You free prisoners and keep faith with those that sleep in the dust ... Who can perform such mighty deeds?

From the Amidah, which is said in all services. This translation comes from the Reform prayerbook. Amidah means 'standing' as it is recited in a standing position. The Talmud says it is the most special prayer.

E

Lord, where shall I find you? High and hidden is your place; And where shall I not find you? The world is full of your glory.

I have sought your nearness, With all my heart I called you, And going out to meet you I found you coming towards me.

Judah Halevi (1075–1141) was a Jewish poet and philosopher who lived in Spain.

F

O God of Your people Israel: You are holy And you have made the Sabbath and the people of Israel holy ... So we have kindled these two lights for love of your daughter, The Sabbath day. Almighty God, grant me and all my loved ones A chance to truly rest on this Sabbath day. May the light of the candles drive out from among us The spirit of anger, the spirit of harm.

From an eastern European Jewish prayer recited by women after lighting the candles on Friday evening

G

On the first day of the year [Rosh Hashanah] it is written [by God], and on the Day of Atonement the decree is sealed ... who shall live and who shall die ... who shall perish by fire and who by water, who by the sword, who by wild beasts, who by hunger and who by thirst; who by earthquake and who by plague, who by strangling and who by stoning ... who shall be tranquil and who shall be harassed ... who shall become poor and who shall wax rich; who shall be brought low and who shall be upraised. But Penitence, Prayer and Charity avert the severe decree.

This prayer is said on Rosh Hashanah (New Year) and Yom Kippur (the Day of Atonement) – called the Days of Awe. Jews pray in synagogue knowing that they have until the end of Yom Kippur before they are judged and their fate for the year is decided – 'sealed'.

ACTIVITY

Your school is to be lent the five paintings below for a travelling Exodus Art Gallery. Your class has been asked to provide each painting with:
a) a title
b) a summary of the part of the Exodus story it shows; look up: Exodus 3.1–10, 7.14–11.5, 14.21 –29, 32.1–20, 34.27–32
c) a description of what God has done, is doing, or is about to do
d) a list of the qualities of God revealed by this episode.

How is God described in the Exodus story?

God is beyond human comprehension. So how can God be described in words? This is one of the oldest problems for all religious believers. You are now going to investigate two contrasting ways of talking about God in the Jewish tradition – on this page the story of Exodus in the Tenakh, and on pages 98–9 the writings of Maimonides.

In the Hebrew Bible ordinary people encounter God. The Bible uses poems and stories to:

- describe how people felt in the presence of God
- compare God to other things
- describe God in human terms that people can understand.

EXODUS ART

1

2

3

DISCUSS

1   Do you think it is helpful or unhelpful to describe God in human terms? Give reasons.
2   The second of the Ten Commandments (Exodus 20.4–6) forbids making images of God. Why do you think this is?
3   Look at pictures 1–5 in the Exodus Art Gallery below. How has each artist depicted God?

One of the most important stories is the Exodus, where Moses leads the Jews out of slavery in Egypt towards the Promised Land. You can read it in Exodus, Chapters 1–20. This story gives a very dramatic impression of God, who is described in human terms. The proper term for this way of talking about God is 'anthropomorphism'.

- God talks regularly to Moses. Moses argues back.
- God hears people crying and decides to help them.
- God gets angry – in fact, furious and vengeful by the end of the story.
- God does some very physical but superhuman things, e.g. sending plagues of frogs etc.; parting the Red Sea so the Israelites can cross it.
- God is moral. God wants people to do right, and not to do wrong.
- God does some cruel things, e.g. killing the Egyptian first-born sons.

There is no doubt that in Exodus God is presented as immanent – doing things in the world and intervening in history to change the course of events.

GALLERY

5

4

How does Maimonides tell us to describe God?

Human comparisons such as the ones in Exodus make God seem very accessible. But this way of looking at God can lead to misunderstandings.

Many Jews are deeply unhappy with this way of looking at God. They want people to see that God is different from any being that we can imagine. They say that God is so transcendent, so beyond this world, and so different from anything that we know that the most significant thing the believer can say about God is that God is indescribable. The person most associated with this view is Maimonides. Maimonides was a philosopher in the Middle Ages. However his views have remained very influential on Jewish ideas about God since then (see Checkpoint).

FOCUS TASK

1 **Describe two Jewish ideas about God:**
 a) as expressed in Exodus
 b) as expressed by Maimonides.
 In your answers make sure you use the words 'immanent' and 'transcendent'. They are explained in the Checkpoint on page 94.
2 **Explain why these contrasting ideas can be helpful to religious believers trying to understand what God is like.**

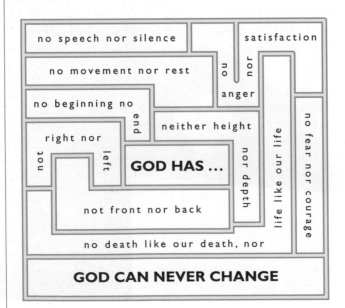

Maimonides made simple

- Maimonides tells us not to take the Bible's language about God literally as God is unknowable.
- God is best described by negatives – by what God is **not**.
- Two of his thirteen principles (see page 11) summarise his ideas.

> I believe in perfect faith that the Creator, blessed be His name, is **one whom no other being resembles**. He alone is our God, now and forever.

> I believe in perfect faith that He the Creator, blessed be His name, **has no physical form and is beyond any form of description.**

> Every time you assert **what God is not** you get closer to true belief. Every time you assert **what God is** you follow your imagination and recede from the true knowledge of God.

THEREFORE GOD HAS . . .

no speech nor silence

no movement nor rest

no beginning no end

right nor left

not

GOD HAS ...

neither height nor depth

satisfaction

no nor anger

life like our life

no fear nor courage

not front nor back

no death like our death, nor

GOD CAN NEVER CHANGE

Maimonides quoted the Bible as a basic source for his beliefs. There is much in the Bible about God being beyond our comprehension. But clearly, the Bible stories also present a far more human idea of God. So how does Maimonides deal with the contradiction?

The Torah speaks in the language of human beings.

We must not take the Biblical descriptions of God at face value. They are used for those who can not cope with abstract ideas. God was kind to use language that even the simplest person would understand, but it must not be taken literally. Whenever God is described as speaking, or having feelings, or physical qualities, do not believe that what we are told is literally true.

The benefits of Maimonides:

This all fits better with my experience

For some people, not having to take the Bible stories at face value is a relief. Many modern Jews find a literal reading of the Bible very hard anyway. They like Maimonides' scientific approach, which fits better with their understanding of the world.

Also, it can strengthen people's faith not to have mistaken mental pictures of God. Some believers, for example, who picture God as an old man in the sky, fixing all that happens to them, can find their faith damaged when something bad happens. Maimonides teaches us not to understand God in this way. After all, in the daily world people have to cope whether or not they see evidence of God acting.

The problem with Maimonides:

If God is so 'other', how on earth can I pray at all?

But there are difficulties.

Why pray to this kind of God? The prayers cannot achieve anything!

And **how** to pray to this kind of God? Our minds are simply not equipped to talk about things beyond the boundaries of our experience. If we are to say anything at all about God we have to use our normal language. Yet none of us wants to be dismissed as 'simple'.

One famous Conservative Jewish thinker, Abraham Joshua Heschel, writing in 20th-century America, agrees with much of what Maimonides wrote, but says, 'This God is all indifference, too "other" to cast a glance at our world.' Heschel is convinced that God is not above human feelings. God is moved by what happens to people. The philosophers may not be able to explain that, but the Jew must believe it.

ACTIVITY

In pairs, role play a conversation between someone who believes God is immanent and personal, and someone who believes God is transcendent and unknowable. In your role play, try to use ideas from the last seven pages.

5.2 How is God revealed to Jews?

✓ CHECKPOINT

Types of revelation

GENERAL REVELATION is indirect and available to everyone. The best example is the natural world. Some religious believers say that the very existence of the Earth and the Universe is evidence of a Creator.

Other examples of general revelation are:

• reason – our God-given ability to work things out for ourselves

• conscience – our God-given inner voice that tells us what is right and wrong.

Some people would say that general revelation is all we need to know truth.

Many others, including most religious believers, tend to disagree with this. General revelation could not, for example, tell you how to live in human society, or how to worship God, why there are suffering and evil in the world, or what will happen to your soul after death.

SPECIAL REVELATION is needed to know these things. Special revelation is God giving special insights directly to a group or individual through an event, a dream, a vision, a prophecy or an experience. Special revelation gives insights that could not be received by general revelation (see main text for examples).

General revelation tends to be similar across the religions, but special revelation creates different religions. Believers in each religion feel they have been given unique insights into God.

. . . in the past?

• The Torah describes how at Mount Sinai Moses received a special revelation (see Checkpoint) from God. God gave Moses the **commandments** which told the Israelites how to worship God and how to live. Most Jews believe these were a special revelation to the Jews.

• The Torah also describes God's special revelation to Jews through **historical events**, such as the Exodus. This revealed to the Jews that God had a plan for them; that they were chosen by God and cared for by God. It revealed that God did not want them to be slaves in Egypt.

• In their wandering through the desert the people of Israel were accompanied by a pillar of cloud by day and a pillar of fire by night. This assured them that the **Shechinah** (the Presence of God) was with them.

• Through early Jewish history **prophets** time and again were given special revelation by God to pass on to the people. Sometimes the messages were specific to that time. For example, Isaiah had revelations that Israel should not ally with the pagan state of Assyria because that would lead to disaster. More often the prophets were called by God to repeat the old messages which people seemed to continually forget: to be faithful to God, worship only the one true God and keep God's commandments.

These events are not just in the past. Jews today feel very closely linked to them as their heritage. One way in which God is revealed today is by remembering and reliving these past events. However, there is a lot more to revelation than this.

. . . in the present?

Religious believers want God to be revealed to them in the present. They don't see religion as being something historical. Over the next eight pages you will examine how important the following channels of revelation are in helping Jews in the modern world to feel connected to God.

FOCUS TASK

1 Copy the diagram above onto a large sheet of paper.

2 As you work through pages 101–8, annotate your diagram with examples of how God is revealed to Jews through each channel of revelation. Be on your guard because these divisions are not watertight. For example, while you are studying revelation through the natural world, you might also gather evidence concerning prayer and meditation or tradition and ritual. You'll find evidence about personal experience throughout.

3 The chart shows these forms of revelation as if they are all of equal importance to Jews. They are not. Part of your task will be to work out which are most important and which are less important in Judaism. At the end you will redraw the pie chart to show what you think is the relative importance to Jews of each segment.

Meeting God in nature

Knowing God through the natural world

Jews believe that God created the world and so the whole world reveals the order, dignity and beauty of its Creator.

Many say that the peace and beauty of the natural world takes them closer to God. The natural world helps them pray.

A

Master of the Universe, grant me the ability to be alone;
may it be my custom to go outdoors each day
among the trees and grass, among all growing things,
and there may I be alone, and enter into prayer
to talk with the One I belong to.
May I express all that is in my heart,
and may all the grasses, trees and plants awake at my coming,
to send the powers of their life into the words of my prayer
so that my prayer and speech are made whole
through the life and spirit of all growing things,
which are made as one by the transcendent source.

Rabbi Nahman of Bratslav (1772–1811). He was a Chasidic rabbi (see page 106).

B

Rather than just look at the calendar I find it helpful to also go outside and observe the moon each night. This helps me reconnect with God's rhythm in nature. The darkness at new moon is like being enfolded by the protective darkness of the womb.

Dr C. Benton, Texas, USA, from his website

Problems

Of course, there are problems with this aspect of revelation. What about suffering, evil and chaos that would appear to be built in as part of the natural order? Is God revealed:

- through natural events such as earthquakes
- through cruelty in the animal world
- through the extinction of the dinosaurs?

This is an issue for discussion which you will return to on page 113.

The cycle of nature

The sense of knowing God through nature is not the most important form of revelation for most Jews. Neither is it unique to Judaism. Believers in almost all religions have recorded similar experiences. However, one aspect which is particular to Judaism is the way the monthly cycle and the celebration of nature at festival times helps Jews to understand and worship God. For example:

Rosh Chodesh (new moon) The Jewish calendar has lunar months. Each month corresponds to a complete cycle of the moon and is welcomed with special prayers (see Source B). Traditionally Rosh Chodesh (the beginning of the month) has been celebrated as a women's festival, because women's natural cycle is close to that of the moon. This has been revived since the 1970s and now many women meet monthly in 'Rosh Chodesh groups' to pray and celebrate among women.

Other examples are Tu B'Shevat, which celebrates the environment (see page 76), Pesach (see page 102) and Succot (a harvest festival).

There are many websites with information about all these Jewish festivals. Try www.jewfaq.org/holiday0.htm.

DISCUSS

1 One Jewish writer said, 'the veils that cover God's reality are often thinner in the natural world than in the man-made world.'
   a) What do you think he means?
   b) Do you agree or disagree? Give reasons.

2 Find out whether any of your class have experienced God through the natural world. If so, do these experiences prove that God exists? Give reasons.

Living traditions

Knowing God through tradition and ritual

Tradition and ritual are very important to Jews. You have already studied the rituals of Shabbat (page 4). Many rituals take place in the home, so children grow up surrounded by their faith.

Through observing the rituals in every detail, all of life becomes worship. As Orthodox Jews think carefully about what they eat (the laws of Kashrut), and wear, and have in their homes, so every act of life can be a dedication of their lives to God. This ensures that for them God is not remote, but involved with everyday life.

Reliving past events

Many rituals re-enact past events. At Pesach (Passover), Jews remember and celebrate their escape from slavery in Egypt (see pages 96–7). According to the Torah, God ordered the Jewish people to relive these events each year: so this festival has been celebrated each year by Jews for thousands of years. It is one of Judaism's most ancient traditions. But it is also a dynamic event which involves all the family in remembering, reliving and reinterpreting the past. The Haggadah (read at the Pesach meal) says that 'in every generation, every Jew should regard himself as if he [or she] personally had come out of Egypt.'

The main features of observing Pesach
- Preparation (see Source D).
- Eight days of celebration in the home and at the synagogue (see Source D).
- On the first two nights there are lavish meals (called seders) incorporating many symbolic elements (see Source C).
- At the seder the story of Passover is retold – in the reading of the Haggadah.
- Songs are sung (Source E, for example).

---

1 **Read Source E. What do you think is the underlying message of this song about:**
   a) suffering
   b) God?

2 **It is not sung at any other time. Why might Jews think it particularly appropriate to sing it at the Pesach seder?**

3 **Pesach is an exciting experience for all who take part. It often makes Jews feel especially close to God. Does this prove that God exists? Give reasons.**

ACTIVITY

1 **Look at Source C. As part of the seder the youngest child present has to ask these four questions:**

a
On all other nights we eat bread or crackers. Why do we eat only matzah on Pesach?

b
On all other nights we eat many kinds of vegetables and herbs. Why do we eat maror at the seder?

c
On all other nights we don't have to dip our food. Why do we dip green herbs in salt water and maror in haroset at the seder?

d
On all other nights we eat sitting up straight. Why do we lean on a pillow tonight?

You are going to go on a guided web search using a worksheet your teacher can give you to find out answers to these questions. To get you started, try this site: www.holidays.net/passover. Record your findings on a table like this:

Ritual/feature	Historical meaning	How it might point Jews to important truths about God

2 **If you get on all right with the first set of questions, here are six more for you to research:**

e
Why is this festival sometimes called 'Passover'?

f
What is the meaning of the word 'Pesach'?

g
Why is the home cleared of all yeast foods before Passover?

h
Why are four glasses of wine drunk at the seder?

i
Why is a fifth glass of wine poured but not drunk?

j
Why is part of a matzah (the Afikomen) hidden, found and then eaten?

C

An egg hard-boiled and roasted: a symbol of sacrifice in the Temple and of new life.

Haroset: chopped nuts, wine, cinnamon and apple representing the mortar that Jewish slaves had to use to build the Pharaoh's palaces.

Parsley: symbol of spring. It is dipped in the **salt water**, which reminds people of the tears of the Jewish slaves when they were in captivity in Egypt.

An example of a seder plate

Shank bone: a symbol of sacrifice. On the first Passover God ordered the Jews to kill a lamb and mark the doorposts of their houses with its blood. When the Angel of Death killed every first-born son in Egypt the Jewish houses could be identified and spared this plague.

Maror: bitter herbs – freshly grated horseradish reflects the bitterness of slavery.

Matzah: this unleavened bread reminds people that the Jews had to leave Egypt in such a hurry their bread did not have time to rise. For the eight days of Pesach Jews eat matzah instead of bread.

D

Pesach	
Preparation	By Passover eve clear the house of all foods containing leavened (fermented) grain products or yeast. Throughout Pesach Jews can neither possess nor eat bread or other foods that contain fermented grain. Grain products that have not fermented are permitted. For example, matzah is made of wheat flour, but it must be put in the oven to bake less than eighteen minutes after the flour comes into contact with the water.
Day 1	The seder (Passover meal). All the laws of Shabbat (see page 17), except the restrictions on cooking and carrying in the street, also apply on this and many other Jewish festivals.
Day 2	Orthodox Jews in the diaspora (outside Israel) have another seder. Reform Jews and Jews in Israel do not.
Days 3–6	Four days of 'half holiday' – when the food restrictions still apply but the Shabbat laws do not.
Days 7–8	Special services are held in the synagogue, and the Shabbat laws apply as on the first two days.

E

One little kid
My father bought for two zuzim.
A cat passed by and ate the kid . . .
A dog arrived and bit the cat that ate the kid . . .
A heavy stick then beat the dog that bit the cat that ate the kid . . .
A fire burned the heavy stick that beat the dog that bit the cat that ate the kid . . .
Water doused the fire that burned the stick that beat the dog that bit the cat that ate the kid . . .
An ox drank all that water up that doused the fire that burned the stick that beat the dog that bit the cat that ate the kid . . .
A butcher slaughtered the same ox that drank the water that doused the fire that burned the stick that beat the dog that bit the cat that ate the kid . . .
The Angel of Death carried off the butcher who slaughtered the ox that drank the water that doused the fire that burned the stick that beat the dog that bit the cat that ate the kid . . .
Then the Holy One Blessed be He killed the Angel of Death who carried off the butcher who slaughtered the ox that drank the water that doused the fire that burned the stick that beat the dog that bit the cat that ate the kid.

The whole evening rounds off with singing, including this song called *One Little Kid.*

DISCUSS

Think back over what you have learned in this course. Find examples of the Torah giving guidance on:
1 God's character
2 an issue of life and death
3 relationships
4 global issues.

The Torah

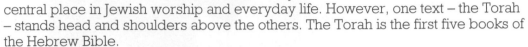

Knowing God through sacred texts

Look back at page 16. You will see that the Jews have many sacred texts. The Jews have been called 'the People of the Book.' Sacred texts are as important a form of revelation as ritual and tradition. They have a central place in Jewish worship and everyday life. However, one text – the Torah – stands head and shoulders above the others. The Torah is the first five books of the Hebrew Bible.

Studying the Torah is a very significant form of revelation. Indeed, some Jews would say that studying the Torah is the most important way God is revealed.

THE TORAH

A powerful symbol of God's presence

For the people of Israel the tablets of stone engraved with the Ten Commandments were a direct link with God and a sign of God's presence among them. They were carried in a special way and given the central place in the Temple. In the same way, the scrolls of the Torah are special today and are a symbol of God's presence. One prayer thanks God for 'giving the glimpse of truth and planting it in the midst of our lives.'

The way Torah scrolls are compiled, decorated, stored and handled in the synagogue today illustrates their great importance. They are handwritten to the strictest standards by trained scribes (see Source J). The scrolls are one of the most expensive items in any synagogue.

A practical guide for the faithful

It will be clear to you from all that you have studied in this book that the Torah is more than just a symbol. As you have seen many times already, it is also the main source of knowledge about God and what God wants. It is the ultimate source of moral authority for Jews (see page 17).

HALACHA refers to the idea of keeping the commandments. Life constantly reveals new situations that Orthodox Jews need to consider in the light of the Torah. New commentaries are always being added, to keep Orthodox Jews up-to-date and suggest how they might follow God's ways in a changing world.

The Torah and other sacred texts also provide a focus for study and meditation.

F

To celebrate his Bar Mitzvah, this boy is reading from the Torah for the first time. He holds a silver pointer as he may not touch the text.

SAVE AS...

A synagogue wants to commission new covers for its Torah scrolls. Write a letter to a designer explaining what the covers say or represent about the Torah.

G

As a rabbi, I have the opportunity to devote a lot of time to studying Jewish texts, and this is a very important spiritual activity in my daily life. The study of any spiritual text is a form of meditation and not simply an intellectual exercise.

Each text has its own spirit waiting to be unlocked. I try to concentrate on the simple meaning of the words and wait for a deeper understanding to appear. This practice affects how I behave and treat other people and gives me inspiration about life.

Paul Glantz (see page 3) is a Masorti rabbi in St Albans, Hertfordshire.

Case study: 'a crystal-clear channel to heaven'

SOFRIM (scribes – singular: SOFER) devote their lives to the work of writing the Torah. In Source J sofer Marc Michaels describes his work.

J

Two rabbis once met and one asked the other, 'My son, what is your work?' The other replied, 'I am a scribe.' The first rabbi said, 'Be careful, because yours is heavenly work. If you leave out one letter, we will find you have destroyed the whole world!'

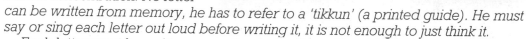

This story shows how the scribe's purpose is to preserve what is understood to be the literal word of God.

The scribe has to have the utmost concentration. No letter can be written from memory, he has to refer to a 'tikkun' (a printed guide). He must say or sing each letter out loud before writing it, it is not enough to just think it.

Each letter must be written according to traditional laws. Even a change as small as a point on a letter can make the work 'pasul' (invalid). A mistake in a name of God cannot be corrected – the whole sheet must be buried or stored away and days of hard work lost.

Each completed sheet must be checked by three rabbis for accuracy, before it can be joined to the scroll. Nowadays the Torah will also go for computer scanning, which can pick up human errors.

The scribe also has to give attention to the materials he uses. The parchment is made from skins that must be prepared, scraped and soaked. Then lines and columns are ruled with a thorn, as no metals can be used as they are symbols of war. The quills are especially cut and used with special black ink made from gallnuts and vitriol. All the materials are natural and hardwearing. Even the sheets of parchment are sewn together with tough animal sinew. It is no job for a vegetarian!

It takes a year to write a Torah scroll, and a celebration is held when it is completed.

The scrolls in use are always treated with great care. They are covered with a decorative velvet or silk embroidered cover or stored in an ornate wooden box. They are handled by manipulating two wooden rollers called 'atsey chayim' (trees of life). A gold, silver or wooden pointer in the shape of a hand (a 'yad') is used while reading to avoid smudging the letters.

However, ink fades or flakes over time and parchment can tear. The sofer checks regularly to repair faded letters and patch holes. Sometimes entire columns are replaced. If even one letter is missing or damaged the whole scroll cannot be used in synagogue services.

Why is such a huge effort made by the scribe? The Bible says in Exodus 15.2 that 'this is my God and I will glorify him.' One scribe explains, 'I try to open a crystal-clear channel to heaven for the congregation, making sure that not one of God's words are changed over the generations.'

Marc Michaels' first project was his own ketubah (wedding contract – see page 45). He then met a sofer who was looking for an apprentice, and has been studying as a sofer ever since. You can find out more about his work as a sofer on his website (www.bayit02.freeserve.co.uk).

1 In what ways is the work of the scribe more than just everyday copying?
2 Explain why Jews put such emphasis on the scribe's art.

H

A sofer at work

I

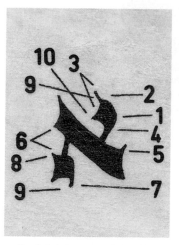

Each letter must be written according to traditional laws. This shows the strokes needed to form just one letter. On Marc Michaels' website you can find out more about the laws a sofer has to follow.

Chasidism

Chasid means 'pious'. Chasidism started as a spiritual revival movement. Its founder, the Ba'al Shem Tov ('Master of the Good Name') (1700–60), said that studying sacred texts was not the only way for God to be revealed. He encouraged joyful worship with singing and dancing. He taught that sadness is a barrier between man and God, but joy opens the way to heaven. He aimed for 'devekus' ('clinging' to God).

The Ba'al Shem Tov said God could be worshipped through everything one did. Asked, 'Where is the dwelling of God?' he answered, 'God dwells wherever man lets him in.' Eating, working, even sex, were spiritual acts if you were aware of God at all times.

He greatly appealed to uneducated Jews. He spread his teachings through stories everybody could understand. He was also a miracle worker and an expert in herbal medicine. He wrote no books.

After his death, his disciples spread his ideas. They were banned, but Chasidism became the strongest form of Judaism in eastern Europe.

Chasidism today

Over 80 per cent of Chasidim were killed in the Shoah. Most survivors moved to other countries, particularly the USA. They keep themselves separate from secular society. They dress traditionally, have separate schools, don't have televisions and do not take jobs that would require them to compromise their dress, beliefs or rituals.

Chasidim have large families and they are the fastest growing sector of Judaism. Many of them regard their survival as the best response to the Shoah. Each child born and each tradition maintained is like a blow to Hitler.

'Lucky to have a rebbe'

In Orthodox and Reform Judaism today a rabbi will be respected because he or she is well educated and is able to understand the traditions and sacred texts of Judaism. By their learning, the rabbi can help ordinary Jews understand more about God. However, most Jews do not put their rabbi on a pedestal. They would be quite suspicious of a rabbi who behaved as if they had some special 'hot-line' to God. However, Chasidic Judaism is different, as you can see from Source K. In Chasidism the 'rebbe' is more in the tradition of the Ba'al Shem Tov (see Checkpoint).

Knowing God through religious leaders

K

I feel more lucky than someone else who may not be a Chasid, and the reason is that we have a rebbe. We have someone that we always look up to and everything in our life is based on what the rebbe tells us to do. We don't take any major or minor decision on our own without asking the rebbe. And we know that the rebbe cares for us.

Chani Lazar, a New York Chasidic Jew

Every Chasid looks upon the rebbe as his own father, as his grandparents. We push and shove to listen to him. We are like one. And he teaches us the past, the Torah, and most often, he makes up songs and he teaches us them. And we sing. It's like everything that he does we're crazy over.

Ben Zion Horowitz, a New York Chasidic Jew

You are brought up to believe that you really are the spiritual elite. I felt very bad for the people who weren't born into the Chasidish lifestyle, you know!

Pearl Gluck a former Chasidic Jew who has now left the community

Pearl came back from seeing the new rebbe, and the girls asked, 'What was He like?' Pearl said He was like Moses coming down from the mountain.

Meyer Schiller, Chasidic Talmud teacher

Interview extracts from *A life apart: Chasidism in America*

Chasidim believe their rebbe is constantly close to God, in a state they call devekus (see Checkpoint). Ordinary Chasidim believe that in the rebbe's presence they can share some of that devekus.

The rebbe is the heartbeat of a Chasidic community – like a 'king', or a national flag. He gives them their identity. The bond may continue even after the rebbe's death. Chasidim pray at their rebbe's grave. They leave notes asking the rebbe to pray for them in heaven.

The rebbe's leadership holds the community together and so gives them the strength to keep themselves separate from the world outside.

✓ CHECKPOINT

Kabbalah

KABBALAH means to receive insight. Kabbalah is Judaism's mystical tradition. A mystic studies or meditates to receive insight that would not be revealed to ordinary believers.

Kabbalah has long been part of the Chasidic tradition. It has also recently become popular with some less orthodox, modern-day Jews, particularly in the USA.

Kabbalah is not intended to be an alternative to traditional Judaism. Kabbalists are supposed to observe their traditional religious duties *but also* practise mystical prayer and meditation. In fact, Maimonides said that no one under 40 should study Kabbalah and even then only after long immersion in the Torah and Talmud. Without this, Kabbalah could lead to magic or heresy.

DISCUSS

1 Goldhamer says, 'God is like a force that cannot be explained intellectually and must be experienced to be known.'
   a) What do you think he means?
   b) Do you agree or disagree? Give reasons.

2 According to Goldhamer, why was he healed?

3 Do you think that Goldhamer's experience proves that God exists? Give your reasons.

4 Do you think that meditations such as Source M are helpful in learning more about God?

'Bringing God within us'

Knowing God through prayer and meditation

Prayer has a significant role for all Jews. Observant Jews pray three services daily in the synagogue: in the morning, afternoon and evening. Praying at set times creates a discipline that can help Jews to stay constantly aware of God. But there are different kinds of prayer.

Rabbi Douglas Goldhamer is a Reform rabbi in Illinois, USA, where his unusual congregation consists largely of deaf people. In his book, *This is for everyone*, he describes experiences that led him to discover the healing power of prayer and meditation.

L

I was raised as an Orthodox Jew. I was taught that God is reached through good works and prayer. I have since learned, through a remarkable series of events, that there is one more step to take.

Twenty-four years ago, I developed crippling pain in my leg. I walked with a cane. The surgeon told me that my left leg would have to be amputated or gangrene would set in within a year, and my right leg might also need to be amputated. I was devastated and frightened.

I prayed to God in the way I had been taught, but my prayers had no effect. I could not accept God saying no so I contacted Hasidic Rabbi Daniel Dresher. He taught me to pray with '*kavannah*' (focus), which eliminates the space between us and God. Praying with *kavannah* is the all-important step beyond faith and good works – to activate God within you. God is like a force that can not be explained intellectually and must be experienced to be known. If we can pray to God within us, instead of God in the heavens, we can begin to eliminate the illness within us.

I added *kavannah* to my prayers for healing and was completely cured in seven months – much to my doctors' astonishment and my joy! I did not need the cane again.

How can we bring God within us? Rabbi Dresher said that if we want to be 'heard' by the Light of the World, we must, as the Shulchan Aruch states, stand before God's Presence, and invite God within us.

One way we can do this is by 'The Candle Meditation' (see Source M), When I do this meditation I can experience God's light within me any time of the day. Don't worry if this doesn't happen right away for you. It took me a while. It is important to practise.

Abridged from the preface to *This is for everyone* by Rabbi Douglas Goldhamer and Melissa Stengel

M

How to bring God inside

Face the lighted candle. The candle represents the Light of God.

There is a 'space' between God's Light and you. You have to eliminate that space to be one with God. In this meditation, you invite the candle to come within you.

With your eyes closed, visualise the candle coming closer and closer towards you. As you do this recite 'The Light of the Lord is my Soul' (Proverbs 20.27) or in Hebrew 'Ner Adonai Nishmat Adam.' Repeat this as a mantra. Focus only on the candle coming inside you until you are filled up with the Light of God.

Through the day, at the water cooler or taking a break from your reading assignment, whatever you may be doing, picture yourself filled with the Light of God. This will give you a connectedness to God that will inspire you.

Abridged from *This is for everyone*. This meditation is from the Zohar – the most important book of the Hebrew Kabbalah (see Checkpoint). Mystics in many religions commonly use light as a symbol of God.

1. How does Felicity Kendall's conversion experience compare with the experience of conversion in other religious traditions you have examined?
2. What attracted Felicity Kendall to Judaism?

Conversion

Judaism does not seek converts, unlike some religions. Indeed, when someone expresses the desire to convert to Judaism they might find many barriers in their way. This is one feature that distinguishes Judaism from Christianity and Islam.

Most people who do convert become Jewish in order to marry a Jewish person, although traditionally this is not considered a good enough reason. However, there are exceptions, as you can see from Source N. You can also see from this that in Judaism conversion is not a one-off experience but a long process of study and discussion, which gradually helps the convert embrace the rituals and traditions of Judaism.

N

There came a time when I was a divorced single mother, living by myself and feeling lost. I felt the need for some kind of spiritual base. Many of my closest friends are Jewish, and they are all bolstered by their faith.

So I rang the rabbi at the West London Synagogue and said: 'I'm really interested in your faith. Can I come and talk to you?' He said: 'There's no point in talking – just come to a service and start from there.' No encouragement which I found surprising, because all you have to say to a Catholic priest is 'I'm interested' and Whoosh you're in!

The next Saturday morning I went along. The congregation was a family and I sensed a tremendous warmth. But I had a lot to learn . . .

I rang the rabbi again. 'Well you'd better read a few books' he said. He rattled off a list. 'Keep coming to the services and if you are still interested in six months, give me a ring.' Six months later he said 'I think you can now join some Hebrew and Bible lessons.' He asked: 'Are you converting because you want to marry someone?' I said no. He said, 'That's good. That means you're serious.'

The classes went on for years because I fell behind in my studies because of my work at the theatre. A wonderful teacher called Mr Smith taught me about the traditions. The female of the family should be the pillar of the house. You have to know all about the Friday night dinner, the prayers, the lighting of the candles, the blessing over the challah, the Passover table, how to keep a kosher home.

You have to go before a board of rabbis who judge if you're fully aware of what is involved, and whether you're ready to go ahead. It only takes half an hour, but I don't think I've ever been more nervous for any audition. However, I passed that test, and so the final step in my conversion was the mikvah (see page 46), which signifies purification. It was beautiful, a glorious sunny day, and I went with my little Catholic Mum from London to Manchester. You go into a building, say the prayers, go under the water, and that's it. You dry your hair, get back on the train, and come back Jewish. It was lovely.

I'm so happy I converted. I feel a tremendous affinity with this religion. I believe in the way that life and death are treated with an up-front acceptance and honesty. Friday night suppers are what I love most; it's a time for the family to get together, and works well with us, except when I'm at work in the theatre. I like a set of rules whereby people know how to behave here and now, not for the hereafter. I could belong here.

Felicity Kendall is a television and stage actress. She was brought up a Catholic but has converted to Judaism. She has since married a Jewish man and has a son who at the time of this interview was approaching his Bar Mitzvah. From *The Mail on Sunday*

FOCUS TASK

1. Redraw the chart from page 100, but resize the pie segments to show how important each form of revelation is to Jews. N.B. There is no single correct answer. The important thing is that in question 5 you can justify your sizing from the evidence in pages 100–108.
2. Put an example of each kind of revelation alongside your chart.
3. Explain whether each one is an example of special revelation or general revelation.
4. Explain how each one might help a Jew to know God better.
5. Finally, write a paragraph explaining the sizes of the segments on your diagram.

5.3 Where was God at Auschwitz?

DISCUSS

**Look at Source A.
Discuss your reactions to
it with a partner.**

1 **What impression
does it give you of the
Nazi accused? Is he
evil or stupid?**
2 **How about the
accusers? Are they
powerful or
powerless?**
3 **Is this a pessimistic or
optimistic picture?
Give reasons.**

✓ CHECKPOINT

The Shoah or Holocaust
The Shoah was the greatest
tragedy of Jewish history.
Between 1941 and 1945 nearly
six million Jews – one third of
world Jewry – were murdered
by the Nazis and their allies in
killing fields, brutal work camps
and places of mass destruction,
such as Auschwitz death camp.
Over 1.5 million children died.
It swallowed up the ancient
Jewish communities of eastern
and western Europe, few of
which emerged unscathed.
British Jews were spared as
Britain was never occupied.

'Holocaust' means
'completely burnt offering'.
When Jews made animal
sacrifices to God in the Temple
in Jerusalem, the Holocaust was
the ultimate sacrifice that could
be made: almost all of it was
consumed by fire and went to
God. Many Jews today prefer to
call the mass slaughter 'Shoah',
meaning 'whirlwind', and used
in the Tenakh to describe
widespread destruction.

1 **Why might some
Jews prefer the
term 'Shoah' to
'Holocaust'?**

A

A cartoon called 'Witnesses for the prosecution', drawn in 1945 when leading Nazis were on
trial for crimes against humanity

In this book the Shoah has been mentioned many times. The events have affected
many aspects of Jews' lives. Look back at the following pages and see how it
figures each time: 27, 37, 60–61 and 106. You should also have studied it in your
history courses as a historical event.

Maybe that is enough for you. Why more? Well, in this final case study, building
on all that you already know about this event, we are going to investigate the
Shoah as a THEOLOGICAL event – which means an event that has affected the way
that many Jews think about God. Some describe the Shoah as a theological and
philosophical watershed: 'Before it we believed this; after it we believed that . . .'
How did different individuals respond to the Shoah? What did they decide about
why God allows suffering? What did it tell them about evil?

A SURVIVOR'S STORY: LEON GREENMAN

Leon Greenman married Else in Stepney Green Synagogue in London in 1935. Else was Dutch. She had been raised by her grandmother who was now very elderly and needed to be cared for, so they decided to move in with her. Leon worked as a bookseller, travelling between London and Rotterdam.

At this time Jewish communities throughout Europe were watching anxiously as the Nazis victimised and persecuted the Jews. Some Jews left Europe if they could. Leon and Else chose to stay in Holland, trusting that there would be no war. When war in Europe did break out in September 1939 they stayed on, but made careful plans to leave Holland should they need to.

On 17 March 1940 their son Barney was born. They registered him as a British citizen at the British Consulate in Rotterdam. Leon and Else registered too. They were told that as British citizens they would be taken back to England if Holland was invaded. Leon gave all-important British passports and their money to Dutch friends for safekeeping.

In May 1940 the Nazis invaded Holland. Their bombs destroyed the centre of Rotterdam. Nazis also brought their anti-Jewish policies into Holland. All Dutch Jews now faced the discrimination and persecution that Jews in Germany had known for years.

Things began to go badly wrong for Leon. His Dutch friends had become scared that the Germans would find the passports and had burnt them. Leon went to the British Consulate. It was abandoned and no one had contacted Leon and Else. They had no proof of their British nationality. Leon's papers were wrongly stamped identifying him as a Dutch Jew.

The Greenman family struggled on as best they could. Then in 1942 Leon was called up for 'Labour in Germany'. On the evening of 8 October 1942 the Greenmans and Else's grandmother were taken from their home and placed on a coach that went from street to street collecting Jewish families. After three months in Westerbok transit camp, on 18 January 1943 they were herded onto a train bound for Poland.

The 36-hour journey, without any food or water, took them right into the heart of Auschwitz-Birkenau, one of the largest Nazi extermination camps.

> I could see Else clearly for she was wearing a thick red cape over her head and shoulders to keep her warm. She could see me also from where she stood, and she gestured a kiss to me, with her hand partly holding up Barney so I could see him too. I will never know just what went through her mind whilst she stood on that wintery platform, perhaps she was happy that the long journey was over.

Fifty men and four or five young women were 'selected' for labour. The rest – approximately 700 men, women and children – were sent straight to the gas chambers. The last time Leon saw his wife and son, they were among other women and children in an open truck.

Out of 750 who arrived at Auschwitz-Birkenau from Westerbok that day, only Leon and one other man were to survive.

For two months Leon stayed at Birkenau, in the quarantine part of this terrible camp. The men experienced horrific beatings, were given menial, useless tasks to do and had to survive on very meagre food rations. They dared not drink the water for fear of contracting dysentery, which took many to hospital and inevitable death.

People in England knew little about the extermination camps, and Leon began to give talks about his experiences. In 1986 he made the first of many trips back to Poland.

> The day of the big 'selection' came. Thousands of us were paraded and stripped. We stood in queues, waiting to pass by the SS officer who gave you a quick glance to see if you were still fit for arduous labour. Those that were, were sent to the right. If you showed weakness you went to the left and on to death in the gas chamber.

Out of thousands of prisoners, 1500 were selected and marched to Auschwitz. Leon was one of the 'selected'. Six months of hard labour, little food, beatings, hangings and floggings went by. A new intake of prisoners included a man who had worked in the administration department at Westerbok. He brought news that documents confirming Leon's British nationality had arrived on the day that he had been deported. He had been called just after the train had departed. But it was too late now.

In January 1945 the Russian Army was approaching Auschwitz, so 10,000 prisoners were forced to march to Gleiwitz, 90 kilometres away. There was no stopping, just walking on in freezing conditions through the snow. Those who could not walk were shot where they fell. Men who attempted to escape were shot. Leon's legs were aching and he stumbled. But he was dragged up by a French prisoner, who risked his own life to help him along.

Some days later the prisoners were moved on again, this time by train. The Germans wanted to get them inside Germany. One hundred and forty men were loaded into each open cattle truck, lying on top of each other. Every day when the train stopped corpses were thrown from the trucks. After five days they arrived at Buchenwald camp in Germany. Those who were still fit enough jumped down from the trucks; those who were too weak were helped to the ground and the dead lay still.

Leon's feet were infected with gangrene. The doctor at Buchenwald was going to amputate them, but Leon pleaded with him. He said he was an Englishman and that the Americans would soon be there. He persuaded the doctor that he only had chilblains. Three months later on 11 April 1945 the American Army liberated the camp at Buchenwald.

Leon was taken to France. He was unable to walk and had to have part of his left foot removed. He arrived back in Rotterdam on 10 October 1945. He was reunited with his father and step-mother but no trace could be found of his Dutch family.

He returned to England and for a while he lived with his two brothers. He received a small government income, but he wanted to support himself so he became a market trader, selling small ornaments. This he did for the next forty years.

'I had to go to Auschwitz to see what was left. To stand in Auschwitz as a free man and say "Look I'm alive," was my way of defeating those who had insulted me all those years ago.'

Leon feels it is more important than ever to fight the prejudice which destroyed his life. At the age of 85 he still campaigns against injustice of all kinds.

> I find it much better to talk openly about this part of my life, because I know that if I hold the feeling inside I would never be able to come to terms with what has happened. I can never forget. My memories on occasion are a little too much to bear.

DISCUSS

1 **In pairs, think about some of the characters in Leon's story. What would you like to ask Leon? Else? Leon's Dutch friends who burnt his passport? The diplomats at the British Consulate? The SS Officer who made the 'selection'? The American soldiers who liberated the camps? The French prisoner who risked his own life to save Leon's?**

2 **Who is to blame for the death of Leon Greenman's family? Share your ideas.**

3 **Where was God while the Nazis were brutally killing people? How do you think a religious believer and a non-believer might answer this question?**

Responding to the Shoah

Theology cannot ignore terrible events like the Shoah. All religious believers, Jews and non-Jews, have to find some way to make sense of it. It poses some very deep questions about the nature of God, the nature of evil and the reasons for suffering. How could God have let this happen? Does the Shoah make it impossible to believe in God? Here are four contrasting Jewish voices.

Richard Rubenstein was an American Jewish theologian who had no personal experience of the events of the Shoah. In the 1960s he wrote about his understanding of the Shoah.

B

Judaism is based on the idea of a covenant between God and the people of Israel. The people agreed to obey His laws, and God would protect and deliver them. Yet how does this work in light of the Holocaust? God does not 'leap into history' to alter events. It seems only logical to conclude that the Jews do not have this special covenant relationship with God. How can we come to any other conclusion since God did not intervene to change the events of the Holocaust? The God of the Jews is the 'Ultimate Nothing'.

Eliezer Berkovits was a leading Orthodox rabbi who lost many members of his family in the Shoah. In his book *With God in Hell* he told moving stories of the religious heroism of people who held firm through the darkest days of the Shoah. Their faith was not destroyed. Neither was his. Berkovits entirely rejected Rubenstein's view (Source B). For him, God *could* not have intervened.

C

Human beings have the freedom to do what they like. We have not been programmed by God only to do good things. Having freedom means human beings can do bad things as well as good things. In the case of the Holocaust these bad things were truly terrible. But some suffering in the world is inevitable because human beings are made this way. People should strive to do good because they choose to.

DOES THE SHOAH MAKE IT IMPOSSIBLE TO BELIEVE IN GOD

Emil Fackenheim was a rabbi in Germany in the 1930s. He spent a short time in a concentration camp in 1938. In the years after the war he wrote about his faith.

D

As Jews we must continue to practise our faith. If we stop practising Judaism, Hitler will have a victory from the grave. We cannot let this happen for we also have a task, a service to the world. Humanity has the ability to 'mend' the world, to restore it as holy and perfect. We Jews must lead the way in this task. God's chosen people will survive and this will be a testimony of life over death, on behalf of all mankind.

Elie Wiesel was deported to Auschwitz as a young teenager. In his book *Night* he said: 'For the survivors, death is not the problem. We learned to live with the death. The problem is to adjust to life.' His accounts of his anger with God are among the most powerful pieces of religious writing to emerge from the Shoah.

E

. . . Never shall I forget those flames which consumed my faith forever.

Never shall I forget that nocturnal silence which deprived me, for all eternity, of the desire to live.

Never shall I forget those moments which murdered my God and my soul and turned my dreams to dust. Never shall I forget these things, even if I am condemned to live as long as God Himself. Never.

✓ CHECKPOINT

Where does evil come from?

The scale of the Shoah forces us to confront this question. Any religious believer must ask 'Where does this evil come from?'

Judaism teaches that God created everything. If so, evil was created by God. If God is omnipotent (all-powerful), evil must be under the control of God. If God is all-loving, we must assume God created evil for a good purpose. So what is that purpose? The answer is to make free will matter. If free will is to mean anything, human beings must have to make real moral choices between good and evil.

What is evil?

In early Jewish texts evil appears in various forms:

- as a **person** – for example, as Satan in the Bible who is created and in the end controlled by God but is opposed to God

- as a **psychological phenomenon** – for example, Haman in the story of Esther has evil as part of his personality. Motivated by jealousy or hatred, he does evil things to God's people.

- as a **force** – for example, in the Kabbalah evil is called the Sitra Achara (the 'other side'). Demonic forces are at war with the forces of good. However, the forces are not equal – evil is subservient to the holy force that created it. The Kabbalah compares the Sitra Achara to a vicious dog on a long lead. When the dog gets out of hand, the owner pulls the lead in. So God will never let evil get out of hand.

However, the most influential thinkers within Judaism will say simply that we do not know what evil is. The more important question is, 'What do we do about it?'

ACTIVITY

1 **Look at these statements. Discuss with a partner which writer or writers of Sources B–E might agree with each statement.**

> 1 The Shoah makes me determined to do good.

> 2 The Shoah makes me angry with God.

> 3 The Shoah makes me determined that Judaism should survive.

> 4 The Shoah makes me doubt the very existence of God.

2 **Now look at these statements. They are more tricky than those in question 1. Which writer or writers of Sources B–E might agree with each statement?**

> 5 God could have stopped the Shoah.

> 6 God could not have stopped the Shoah.

3 **Do you think that the fact that Rubenstein (Source B) did not actually experience the Shoah makes his view less important than the views of the other three writers?**

SAVE AS...

4 *Either* Which writer do you most agree with? List them from 1 to 4 putting the one you agree with most as number 1 and the one you agree with least as number 4. Write a paragraph to explain your choice.
or If you disagree with all of the writers, write a paragraph which best explains your own view as to how the Shoah should affect belief in God and why you do not agree with any of the other points of view.

What do Jews do about evil?

For Jews it is important to struggle against evil by total obedience to God. If all people followed God's commandments, evil would be restrained and powerless.

In the Shoah individuals had to choose between good and evil. The massive evil of the Shoah was only possible because too many people chose evil and not enough chose good. Evil will lead to suffering. Unrestrained evil will lead to unrestrained suffering.

Suffering

Suffering comes from two different sources: human-made (for example the Shoah, a result of evil) and natural (for example floods or earthquakes, products of the physical world). For religious believers, suffering raises the question, 'How can an all-loving and omnipotent God let suffering happen?' This question is explored in the Bible in the book of Job. Job, a good man, endures much suffering. Two possible explanations are considered:

- suffering is God's way of testing Job's faith
- suffering is a punishment for Job's sins.

Both explanations are rejected: Suffering is part of God's plan. Human beings cannot understand it but must accept it. The question 'Why do the good suffer?' should not be asked. In Ethics of the Fathers, Rabbi Yannai says, 'It is not in our power to explain either the well-being of the wicked or the sufferings of the righteous' (4.15). Most other Jewish writers agree with this view.

Much suffering is caused by the forces of nature and some teachers argue that humans must learn to live within the balance of nature as it is not in God's will to tilt this balance. The important issue again is how we respond to suffering.

Historically, rabbis have interpreted suffering as an opportunity to deepen their obedience to God. Rabbi Akiva famously recited the Shema with deep joy when being tortured by his Roman captors, and on trial for his life. He explained he felt that for the first time in his life he was able to put his soul into the prayer because this time it could cost him his life. It was a chance to love God unconditionally. He did not resent his suffering. He did not need to look for a reward in the next life in exchange for suffering. He welcomed the closeness to God it created in this life.

FOCUS TASK

Write a reply to this letter explaining your own beliefs about the best way to learn from the Shoah. If you prefer you could present this as a poem or a drawing.

DISCUSS

Read the checkpoints on page 113. Why did God allow the dog such a long leash in the Shoah?

Dear Teacher

I am a survivor of a concentration camp.

My eyes have seen what no man should witness:

Gas chambers built by learned engineers,

Children poisoned by educated physicians,

Infants killed by trained nurses,

Women and babies shot and burned by high school and college graduates.

So I am suspicious of education.

My request is: Help your students become human.

Your efforts must never produce learned monsters, skilled psychopaths, educated Eichmanns.

Reading, writing and arithmetic are important only if they serve to make our children more human.

Learning from the Shoah

Many people see Shoah education as an essential part of the curriculum. By facing head-on the issues that led to the Shoah they believe that people can prevent such an event happening again. Here are some of the issues:

1 Can you think of at least three reasons why the idea of 'untermenschen' is wrong?

2 How can religious beliefs help believers resist racism? You might want to look back at page 57.

3 How does Steven Spielberg think the stories of Holocaust survivors can eradicate intolerance?

4 Do you think the Holocaust should still be remembered and taught? Discuss as a class or in pairs.

Issue 1: racism – how can we resist the forces of racism?

Nazism denied that people all share a common humanity. Nazis divided people into racial groups and stated that some were better than others. Slavs, Africans, Romanies and Jews were 'untermenschen' (racially inferior). This racism was used to justify discrimination and mass murder. Wherever racist views exist, the potential for another Shoah also exists.

F

Schindler's List *was just a little stone that started a big avalanche – the Shoah Foundation.*

This archive will be an on-line living documentary. Each face you see is a life. I feel this needs to be taught in schools, to eradicate hatred and intolerance in its various forms. People have to learn that we are all the same.

Steven Spielberg set up his Shoah Foundation as a result of making *Schindler's List*, in 1994. The Foundation aims to record the stories of survivors, by recording their firsthand evidence for researchers and educators to use in the future. The project is the largest undertaking of its kind. Over 50,000 interviews of two to five hours each have been conducted, in 31 languages and 57 countries. Participants are mostly Jews but there are also non-Jewish homosexuals, gypsies, liberators and rescuers. Steven Spielberg has put a lot of his own money into creating this project. Each interview costs $1000 to record. The archive will eventually be made available for research through documentaries, CD-ROMs and books.

5 What do you think Elie Wiesel meant by the statement in Source H?
6 Why do you think countries were slow to help Jewish refugees?
7 How far can countries who refuse to take refugees be held responsible for what happens to them?
8 Read Source I. Did Jews living in the 'Free World' have a particular responsibility to help their fellow Jews? Give reasons.
9 How can religious beliefs help people who are being persecuted? You might want to look back at page 112.

Issue 2: asylum – how can we help persecuted peoples?

When Jews tried to flee from Germany in the 1930s, country after country refused them sanctuary. Some governments simply refused to take them in, or took only a few. There are many harrowing stories of people, even young children, being returned to the hands of the Nazis and so to the death camps. Many were left bewildered and alone, while countries, including Britain, admitted only some of those applying for refuge and slowed the process with excessive paperwork.

G

European Jewry was ground to death between the twin millstones of a murderous Nazi intent and a callous Allied indifference.

Henry Feingold, 1970

H

The opposite of love is not hate, it is indifference.

Elie Wiesel

I

We cannot understand how you can eat and drink, how you can rest in your beds, how you can stroll in the streets and I am sure you are doing all those things – while this responsibility rests on you. We have been crying for months and you have been doing nothing.

Rabbi Weissmandel of Bratislava speaking during the Second World War about Jews living in the 'Free World'.

10 How do people react to laws which their conscience tells them are wrong? How should they react?
11 Is patriotism a virtue? To what extent is it morally right to take pride in one's country?
12 Many individuals involved in the Holocaust defended themselves by saying they were simply obeying orders. Do you think this is a satisfactory defence?
13 How can their beliefs help religious believers decide when to obey authority and when not to? You might want to look back to page 64.

Issue 3: personal moral responsibility – is obedience a bad thing?

One explanation is that the Holocaust happened because Hitler chose to do harm on a massive scale. But Hitler was only one man. His ability to do evil alone was limited. His fellow Nazis made his awful plan a reality. A fuller explanation is that the Holocaust happened because thousands of ordinary people – lawyers, policemen, train drivers, doctors and civil servants – joined Hitler in his destruction, and millions of others allowed themselves to be frightened or shamed into saying and doing nothing. Hundreds of thousands simply got on with 'their duty', not questioning whether it was morally right.

Education in Nazi Germany tried to indoctrinate young people to obey the Nazi leadership. Individuality, personal expression and critical awareness were all discouraged. Adolf Hitler said, 'The weak must be chiselled away. Young people will grow up who will frighten the world. I want a violent, arrogant, unafraid, cruel youth who must be able to suffer pain.'

5.4   The Messianic age

Around 2500 years ago, the Jewish people were in despair. Many Jews had been forced to leave Israel and were in exile (see page 7). The prophets had a reassuring message for them: if they were faithful and worshipped God, then God would send a Messiah to start a new age on Earth.

This Messiah will not be God, but he will be an exceptional human being. He will be righteous, he will be wise and he will be a great leader. He will be descended from King David – the most successful king of Israel. When the Messiah comes, the Jews will be able to return to Israel, all people will worship the one true God and there will be peace on Earth. According to Isaiah's vision, at the time even the animal world will live in peace: 'the wolf shall dwell with the lamb' (Isaiah 11.6 – see page 85).

This is a powerful idea and has inspired many Jews through the centuries since. The Tenakh nowhere says **when** this Messiah will come and gives no sure signs by which people will recognise the Messiah. This has not stopped people looking for signs. In fact, the Christian religion began as an offshoot from Judaism because some Jews thought that Jesus was the promised Messiah.

Many Jews today still hope for the Messiah to come. Orthodox Jews expect a literal Messiah – a person with all the qualities promised by the prophets. Most Reform Jews don't take it literally. For them the Messiah is not an individual, but a symbol. They hope for a time when all people will work together to bring the Messianic age to Earth. At this time government worldwide will be fair and just. Relationships will be mended. Morality will be restored. People of different faiths will work together to the same ends.

DISCUSS

1   **What do Jews mean by 'the Messianic Age'?**

2   **Choose one line from Source A that especially appeals to you.**

3   **Write your own vision of what a future that has these qualities will really be like.**

4   **Find two newspaper articles:**
    a) **one that illustrates an example of this happening in the world today**
    b) **one that illustrates the opposite of this happening.**

5   **'Source A is an idealistic vision of the future that can never happen.'**
    Explain whether you agree or disagree with this statement, showing you have considered other points of view.

A

And then all that has divided us will merge

And then compassion will be wedded to power

And then softness will come to a world that is harsh and unkind

And then both men and women will be gentle

And then both women and men will be strong

And then no person will be subject to another's will

And then all will be rich and free and varied

And then the greed of some will give way to the needs of many

And then all will share equally in the earth's abundance

And then all will care for the sick and the weak and the old

And then all will nourish the young

And then all will cherish life's creatures

And then all will live in harmony with each other and the earth

And then everywhere will be called Eden once again.

Judy Chicago Merger: 'A Vision of the Future' (late 20th century)

Thinking about God – Review tasks

A

1 What story is shown in the picture?
2 What qualities of God are highlighted in this story?
3 a) Explain in your own words what the Jewish writer Maimonides thought was wrong with anthropomorphism.
   b) Explain how far you agree with this statement, showing that you have considered another point of view.

B

1 Define the terms:
   a) 'special revelation'
   b) 'general revelation'.
2 State whether the Ten Commandments are an example of special revelation or general revelation. Explain your answer carefully.
3 'Studying the Torah is the best way to know God.'
   Explain how far a Jewish person might agree with this, showing that you have considered different viewpoints within Judaism.

C

1 This sculpture is a memorial to those who died in the Shoah. What was the Shoah?
2 Explain why Jews prefer the term 'Shoah' to the word 'Holocaust' to describe these events.
3 Describe how the artist who created this sculpture has attempted to convey the suffering of those who died in the Shoah.
4 'The suffering of the Jewish people during the Shoah makes it impossible to believe in God.'
   Explain how far you agree with this statement, showing that you have considered another point of view.

Conclusion

You've reached the end of your course. How will it be useful to you?

Your exam

Your chief concern is probably to get a good grade in your exam. We have helped you in various ways. Here is a reminder of the ideas you will need to bear in mind when you revise for your exam.

Different traditions

Jews hold a range of views. In your exam, you will need to show that you understand how and why different Jews have different attitudes to moral and theological issues.

You will improve your grade if you can show your grasp of the differences between Jewish traditions, or between Judaism and another religion, on moral issues.

Sources of authority

You have examined the ways Jews use sources such as the Torah and Talmud or their religious leaders as authorities.

You will improve your grade if you can not only name the sources of authority used by Jews, but also show how different Jews use each source of authority.

Absolute and relative

You have investigated the difference between an absolute approach to morality and a relative approach and have recorded your own examples of absolute and relative responses to different issues.

You will improve your grade if you can refer to absolute and relative morality confidently. You should show you understand that they are not watertight definitions; rather, they show an 'approach' to decision-making on certain issues by certain traditions.

Core beliefs

You have studied some of the core beliefs that lie at the heart of Jewish thinking on moral issues.

You will improve your grade if you can not only describe such beliefs, but also explain and demonstrate how these beliefs inspire Jews and affect their values and their actions. Judaism is a living faith, evolving year by year as its followers meet new challenges. This course is about real-life Judaism. It is your understanding of the relationship between these beliefs and Jewish values and actions that will interest the examiner.

Your own views

This course has given you plenty of opportunity to express your own views and to give reasons for them. You may be surprised that even this will be useful in your exam.

Sometimes you are specifically asked for your view in an exam question. The reasons for your opinion, and your ability to back it up, interest the examiner more than the viewpoint itself. So, remember: you will improve your grade if you can express your own views on issues you have tackled, and explain and support them with reference to the Jewish ideas you have studied in this book.

Your beliefs and values

One of the aims of Religious Education is to learn from religion. Religion gives its followers beliefs and values to live by. This course has encouraged you to debate, to understand and to make your own decisions about Jewish beliefs and values. The beliefs and values you have studied in this course may be similar to your own or they may be different. In either case, this course should have helped you to clarify your own beliefs and values.

RE-EVALUATION

On page 5 of this book you recorded your own views on the relevance of studying Judaism. Has your view changed at all? If so, how and why?

On page 22 you thought about the values that are important to Jews. Look back at the four sentences you wrote and see whether you now want to change anything. If so, how and why?

FOCUS TASK

The illustration shows some values that Jews might think are important to help guide people in their moral decision-making.

1 Choose three that you would like to take with you into the future. Explain your choice.
2 Explain whether you reject any of the values altogether and, if so, why.
3 For your three chosen values, give an example of how they might affect your actions in the future.

Glossary

Many of the words in this glossary are Hebrew words. They have been written using English letters but, as Hebrew uses a different alphabet, you may see them spelled differently in other places. We have tried to spell them in a way that will help you to say them, but be aware that English-speaking Jews differ in their pronunciation, especially in which syllable they stress.

abortion (1) the termination of a pregnancy before the fetus is sufficiently developed to survive
(2) operation to cause this

absolute morality belief that there is a right course of action in a moral dilemma that is true for all situations

agnostic someone who says it is not possible to know whether a god exists

agunah (plural: agunot) 'chained woman', unable to remarry because her husband will not grant her a divorce

Amidah 'standing'; prayer said standing as part of all services

anti-Semitism prejudice or discrimination against Jews

assimilation 'becoming similar'; Jews who abandon Jewish traditions to become more like people in the host country are said to assimilate

atheist someone who does not believe there is a god

Bar Mitzvah 'son of the commandment'; a Jewish boy is considered an adult when he reaches the age of thirteen; ceremony and celebration when a boy aged thirteen and is called to read from the Torah for the first time

Bat Mitzvah 'daughter of the commandment'; a Jewish girl is considered an adult when she reaches the age of twelve (Orthodox) or thirteen (Reform); depending on whether she is Orthodox or Reform she may have a ceremony and celebration and be called to read from the Torah for the first time

bedeken 'veiling' – the groom confirms the identity of the bride before covering her face with a veil for the wedding ceremony

Bet Chayim 'house of life' – cemetery

Bet Olam 'house of eternity' – cemetery

brit/brit milah circumcision

capital punishment killing someone as punishment

challah (plural: challot) bread, traditionally plaited or round, for Shabbat and festival meals

Chanukah festival of lights lasting eight days

cheder Jewish religion school on Sunday morning; may have midweek session(s)

chevra kadisha burial society

chupah wedding canopy; also used to refer to the wedding ceremony

covenant a pact between two parties; refers to the special relationship God formed with Abraham

diaspora outside Israel

discrimination the action of treating someone unfairly because of a prejudice

Erev 'evening' or 'eve' – the daytime of the day leading up to Shabbat and festivals

euthanasia ending a person's life deliberately but for compassionate reasons to end suffering:
(1) active – something is done to a person, e.g. they are given drugs, to make them die more quickly
(2) compulsory/involuntary – someone else, e.g. a doctor or family member, decides it would be in a person's best interests to end their life
(3) passive – any form of treatment that might extend a person's life is taken away, e.g. a life-support machine is turned off
(4) voluntary – a person asks for their life to be ended

Gemara commentary on the Mishnah, included in the Talmud

general revelation indirect revelation about God available to everyone; truths about God revealed through the natural world, through reason, through conscience or through moral sense

get document of divorce

haggadah 'telling' – book used at seder

halacha (from the root 'to go') refers to the entire range of Jewish law and practice, including religious, social, familial and personal obligations

immanent 'present in the universe' – describes God as acting in human affairs and affecting human life

impersonal an impersonal God is more like an abstract force than like a person

Kabbalah Jewish mysticism

Kabbalists Jews concerned with mysticism

Kaddish 'making holy' – prayer said by mourners and in synagogue services

ketubah marriage document received by the bride from the groom and signed by both

Kiddush 'making holy' – prayer, usually said over wine, to declare the holiness of Shabbat and festivals

kosher in accordance with Jewish law; mostly used with reference to food

Masorti 'traditional'; Jews who believe the Torah was inspired by God and developed historically, rather than given complete to Moses by God. Masorti Jews believe that the laws and traditions still have relevance today

matzah unleavened bread eaten at Pesach

menorah either the seven-branched candlestick originally used in the Temple or the nine-branched candlestick used on Chanukah, also called 'chanukiah'

Messiah a hoped-for saviour of the world

mezuzah parchment containing the Shema, which is put in a small container to be fixed on the doorposts of Jewish homes

Midrash rabbinic commentary and interpretation of Torah

mikvah ritual bath for spiritual cleansing

Milchemet mitzvah obligatory war

Milchemet reshut optional war

Mishnah the Oral law; commentary on the Torah, written down around 200CE; included in the Talmud

mitzvah (plural: mitzvot) commandment or duty; also refers to any good deed

mohel person who performs brit milah

monotheism believing in one God; Judaism is a monotheistic religion

Orthodox Jews who believe God gave the complete Torah to Moses, and therefore live according to Jewish laws and traditions

personal a personal God seems close to believers and has some human qualities

pogrom organised massacre of Russian Jews in the late nineteenth century

polytheism believing in more than one god; Judaism is not a polytheistic religion

prejudice the attitude of having an opinion that is not based on fact

rabbi 'my master' – an authorised Jewish teacher. Traditionally leads a synagogue community with regard to spiritual and Jewish legal matters

Reform Jews who believe the Torah was inspired by God and developed historically, rather than being given complete to Moses by God. Reform Jews will set aside Jewish laws and traditions that they feel are not relevant to modern life

relative morality belief that different situations require different courses of action

sanctity of life belief that life is holy or sacred

secular to do with everyday life and affairs of this world

seder 'order'; traditional Jewish evening service for Pesach, including reading the Haggadah and eating special symbolic foods; also used by some to describe ceremony with foods for Tu B'Shevat

Sefer Torah Torah scroll

Shabbat weekly day of holy rest beginning at sunset on Friday and ending after dark on Saturday. Special synagogue services are held and Orthodox Jews do no work

Shabbat Shalom 'peace be to you on the Sabbath' – Shabbat greeting

Shacharit morning service

shadchan matchmaker

shalom 'peace' or 'wholeness'; also Hebrew for 'hello' and 'goodbye'

Shechinah the Presence of God

shechita Jewish ritual slaughter of animals whose meat is to be eaten

Shema statement of Jewish beliefs about God, from Deuteronomy Chapters 6 and 11. It is said as a prayer as part of daily services and included in a mezuzah and tephilin

shiur study session

shiva seven days 'sitting' observed by mourners immediately after the funeral

Shoah 'calamity' – Hebrew term used by Jews to refer to the Holocaust

shul 'synagogue'; this Yiddish word is the usual way most British Jews refer to synagogue

sofer (plural: sofrim) scribe

special revelation direct revelation about God to an individual or group, e.g. the Torah was revealed to Moses; gives insights into the will or nature of God through, for example, a dream, vision, prophecy or experience

tallit prayer shawl

Talmud Mishnah and Gemara with further commentaries

tefilah prayer

Tenakh The Jewish Bible (stands for Torah, Neviim, Ketuvim, see page 16)

tephilin small boxes, worn on the forehead and arm for weekday morning prayers, containing the Shema and other passages from the Torah

theological to do with the nature of God

Torah 'law' or 'teaching'; usually refers to the first five books of the Bible

transcendent 'outside the created universe' – describes God as not limited by the rules of nature or time that affect human beings

Tu B'Shevat New Year of the Trees

tzedakah doing righteous acts – refers to charitable deeds and donations

tzizit specially knotted fringes on the corners of a tallit, and on the undergarment worn by Orthodox Jewish males

Yarzheit 'year-time' – the anniversary of a death; the candle lit to mark the anniversary of a death, also lit on Yom Kippur

Yom Hashoah 'Holocaust Day' – day of remembrance for those who died in the Shoah

Yom Kippur 'Day of Atonement' – day of fasting and prayer for forgiveness

Index